DON CUPITT

THE WORLD TO COME

SCM PRESS LTD

334 01815 3

First published 1982
by SCM Press Ltd
58 Bloomsbury Street, London WC1

Phototypeset by Input Typesetting Ltd, London
and printed in Great Britain by
Richard Clay Ltd (The Chaucer Press)
Bungay, Suffolk

The World to Come

Contents

Introduction

In prose much too purple to be quoted *verbatim*, Bertrand Russell once threw down a challenge. It is now almost certain, he said, that we live in a universe completely devoid of meaning or purpose, a universe that has brought us into being by a string of accidents and that in the end offers us no better prospect than individual extinction in the grave and eventual corporate extinction as a species. From now on any philosophy of life that can hope to stand will have to reckon with these facts and to show how human ideals can be preserved in the face of them.[1]

How many religious writers have yet taken up Russell's challenge? Few or none, because for a long time now most religious thought has been absorbed in a rearguard action, preoccupied with the basically political task of trying to save as much as possible of an ancient system of thought and its associated institutions. Theologians are classified as conservative, liberal or radical according to how much they think can be salvaged, and this over-riding political preoccupation makes us forget that the great philosophers and religious innovators of antiquity had followed Russell's method, not ours. They began with a diagnosis of the human condition as it appeared to them, and recommended a way of life that would be an appropriate response to the truth. Russell is surely right to say that it is time we attempted something similar today, for it is the case that during the nineteenth century a new understanding of man's place in the universe developed, prevailed, and now sets the agenda for modern thought. It has a traceable ancestry, for as Russell's own style reminds us, it owes something to ancient Epicureanism and Scepticism; but its modern form is sufficiently new and disturbing to have caused a considerable shock in late-Victorian times.

However, before taking up the challenge we need to qualify Russell's picture of the human situation. The new account really has two main themes, the one from the natural sciences that he mentions, and another arising from the development of critical thinking. We need to grasp the relation between the two if we are to understand clearly where we are now, and why.

The scientific theme is indeed much as Russell describes it, and modern man does find himself landed with a very unfriendly cosmology. Our highly refined and elegant scientific world-picture carries the clear implication that our moralities, art and religions are purely human constructions that are in no way endorsed by the universe at large. Russell saw this as a reason for taking a tragic view of life, but in the calmer atmosphere of eighty years later we can now see that it was also the inevitable corollary of the way science had developed. Modern science had after all set out to expel ideas of purpose and value from nature since its very beginnings. The completion of this process was delayed, and in the early nineteenth century science was still residually theological, but between the 1830s and the 1870s it at last became fully and finally professionalized, autonomous, secular and positive.[2] All remaining theological elements dropped out, and the result was the 'meaningless' universe in which we now have to live. Russell wrote at a time when the history of science had hardly got going as a subject, and he talked as if the bleakness of the modern picture of man's place in the universe was just a factual discovery. Maybe it was, and maybe not; but at any rate we have to reckon with the fact that it was also a cultural creation with a fully explicable history which is much better understood now than it was in Russell's day.

So alongside the late-Victorian realization of the coldness of the scientific world-picture we need to set another realization, which is both related to and yet in some ways in conflict with it. As ideas of meaning and value were withdrawn from nature they became concentrated within the human realm, and Western thinking became steadily more man-centred or anthropocentric. Through critical philosophy and philosophy of language, and through the development of history and the social sciences, it came to be realized how completely we are enclosed within the limits of our own humanity, bound by history, culture and language, and able to see the world only from a human point of view which is itself perpetually shifting. We can have no absolute knowledge,[3] and may count ourselves fortunate if we can justify our claims to possess some objective knowledge of the world.

The first realization was Copernican in spirit, for it suggested that although we have a natural and childish tendency to see everything as revolving around ourselves and as existing for our sakes, the truth is rather that we are marginal in the cosmos. During the Victorian period the steady extension of the cosmic time-scale and the triumph of Darwinism rammed home the Copernican lesson: man is wholly a product of nature and has no objective reason for claiming any special significance in nature. But the second realization was anti-Copernican, for it suggested that the human world in all its manifold expressions is all there is for us. The typical art-form of the period, the naturalistic novel, shows the implications of this complete anthropocentrism, for the novel is concerned solely with human reality. Unlike myth and epic, and unlike even natural science and ideology, it does not view the human world and weigh it in the light of an external and superhuman perspective or order of meanings and purposes. For it the human world is simply *the* world, the primary world, of which religion, science and so forth are merely specialized offshoots.

It seems, then, that modern experience has two poles.[4] Objectively it is Copernican, and subjectively it is anthropocentric. If we can justify the objectivity of scientific knowledge, then the Copernican vision will have the greater weight, but if we are obliged to adopt a merely instrumentalist view of science, then the anthropocentric vision will be the stronger. On both accounts religion, morality and art will be seen as human cultural products, but our attitude to them will be slightly different if we think that science really does give us some objective knowledge of reality from what it will be if we have to conclude that scientific thinking is just as much bound by human interests and limitations as is any other cultural activity.

If science does give us objective knowledge, then it would seem appropriate for us to be rather strict scientific rationalists who trust only science, and the philosophy of science inasmuch as it proves the objectivity of science. In that case we will probably have a rather apolitical, uncommitted and ironical attitude to all other human concerns. Training in the scientific method will create in us a dispassionate and objective spirituality that is simply not very interested in ourselves, the problems of our own existence and our own destiny. Only objective knowledge matters, and the individual does not matter. But then we face the difficulty that such an outlook is possible only for a small élite and cannot be generalized to provide a whole society with a framework to live by. For if scientific knowledge is the only real knowledge we have, and people at large come to realize this, then the intellectual nakedness of the moral, religious and political beliefs that most people live by will be painfully exposed. If in all the affairs that most matter to people in their social life there is no objective court of appeal, then it would seem that we will be for ever at the mercy of feelings and fashions and an interminable struggle for power.

Alternatively, if science be seen as just one human cultural activity among others and the anthropocentric point of view prevails, then the basic human activities of science, art, religion, morality and politics will all be pursued in much the same spirit. Each language-game will be seen as having its own rules and will be played as long as the participants find it worth playing. Pragmatism will prevail. From an anthropocentric point of view each activity has a contribution to make to human well-being and each may be cultivated as such, though against a general background of metaphysical agnosticism which will of course commit us to a man-centred view of religion.

I suspect that the issue between the two views of scientific knowledge is one of those perennial philosophical issues which will never be finally settled because we are in no position to settle it. How could a scientific realist ever prove his point by setting scientific theory and objective natural structures side by side and demonstrating their point-by-point correspondence? Nobody disputes that gravitational theory enables us to get certain sums right and make some successful predictions, but from what point of view could we possibly acquire such a direct, intuitive and unmistakable acquaintance with the gravitational force that we would be fully entitled to assert that the theory of gravity is objectively true of reality? We cannot imagine what it would be like to have immediate knowledge of a natural force and its properties. And if we cannot say clearly how the issue between the two views of science could be decided, then the balance of the argument tilts in favour of anthropocentrism, which allows for the undecidability. Realism, if still held, becomes an intellectual act of faith which is unable to prove its own truth. Either way, be it noted, religion loses its old realist sort of truth and human life can no longer be objectively appraised against the background of a rich and 'meaningful' vision of the sacred cosmic order. If scientific realism is true, then the old sacred cosmologies are now known to be false. If anthropocentrism is true, then science is one useful human language-game and religion is another, but both are human constructions: the sacred vision is no longer an *independent* witness and guarantor of human concerns.

So modern culture hangs uncomfortably suspended between a Copernican point of view for which the human is ultimately insignificant, and an anthropocentric point of view from which it is all there is for us. Not surprisingly, as people began to grasp the implications of this new understanding of the human condition, they reacted in ways ranging from the blackest pessimism to the most optimistic secular humanism. One can see the contrasting responses early on, in such figures as Schopenhauer and the young Marx. But on one point there was agreement: acceptance of the new vision was thought to make Christian faith no longer a live option. It was assumed that as the truth became more widely known traditional religion would break down and disappear. Some might lament this and others might rejoice at it, but there was a general feeling of inevitability. The reason was that the Western tradition had long understood religion in terms that were both very metaphysical and very eudaemonistic.[5] Christianity seemed wholly committed to the claims that absolute knowledge was possible, that the church possessed it, and that it consisted in the good news that human beings really do occupy a uniquely-important position in the whole cosmic scheme of things. The church seemed to claim that it is factually true that my origin, my whole life and my destiny are in the hands of a benign and all-powerful supernatural Person, and indeed that the whole universe is run by a Person for the benefit of persons. The claim to absolute knowledge and the throughgoing eudaemonism would have been bad enough separately; combined, they seem absurd. Accordingly, those who saw the human condition most clearly could find little in religion but illusion and a flight from reality.

There was, however, one obvious exception. Long ago the
Buddha had presented a view of man and of the human condition
that is remarkably cool and disenchanted and that in some ways
anticipates the modern view, and he had then gone on to prescribe
a spirituality and a way of life that he saw as an appropriate
response to and remedy for it. His example suggests that it might
be possible for us in our time to work out a philosophy of life and
a form of religious practice that represent a genuinely truthful
response to the human condition as we now perceive it. We will
probably not be able to follow the Buddha's own path for,
attractive though it is to many Westerners, we are in the end not
Buddhists but products of the Christian tradition. For us the more
likely course is to draw encouragement from the Buddha's example and seek to reinterpret Christian faith in such a way as to
free it from the fantasies of absolute knowledge and of eudaemonism. One might, for example, come to regard Christianity as
a language-game with an associated way of life that deserves to be
pursued just for its own sake.

Modern theologians are sometimes asked why, if Christianity
is not descriptively true in the old supernaturalist and realist sense
and needs radical revision, one should seek to cling on to it at all.
Why not simply abandon religion? But this comment underesti-
mates the sheer magnitude of the cultural crisis into which we
have been sliding for the past two centuries or so. Various
nineteenth-century prophets saw it coming: Dostoyevsky, for
example, in the saying, 'If God is dead, everything is permitted.'
For historical reasons we have become so habituated to drawing
our ethic, our spiritual stance and our sense of life's meaning and
goal from an authoritative vision of an objective sacred order,
that when that order breaks down it appears to bring everything,
but *everything*, else down with it. Up to a century or so ago only
a few intellectuals knew the bad news. They might be sceptics and
pessimists, but their dinners continued to be served because their
servants had not yet heard the bad news. Today, word has gone
round. Popular beliefs flourish, but with an unmistakable air of
unease and bad conscience. We all know that the old foundations
of the moral order are gone. The breakdown of the old sacred
cosmology that underpinned the moral order has left modern
society with no agreed moral theory and no agreed method of
settling moral questions, and Christians are in no better case, for

they are as much divided among themselves as is society at large. But if we cannot find an objective court of appeal that really can settle moral disputes, are we willing to accept the implication that in the end the only judges are fashion and force? We cannot, for society cannot hold together internally, and in the present state of weaponry international relations cannot be safely conducted, on a basis of moral scepticism. Confined to a small élite, moral scepticism may not be too serious a matter, but when it becomes widely diffused many individuals find it too hard to bear and social life begins to disintegrate.

One common and understandable reaction is to reject critical thinking and the scepticism that it has produced, and revert to some form of dogmatism. But the scepticism will still be there underneath, for the history of the past few centuries cannot be undone; and neo-fundamentalism is a cure worse than the disease, for it is fanatical, intolerant, irrational and war-mongering. It is a kind of spiritual fascism.

If we cannot go back, is it possible to go forward and find something better on the far side of modern nihilism? I believe it is, though the way is hard. Put at its simplest, the task is to learn to practise religion just for its own sake, disinterestedly, and to become a creator rather than a passive recipient of religious meaning and value. A world in which people have become active creators of religious value is what I mean by the Kingdom of God.

There are various stages here. First Christianity has to be purged of its objective supernatural apparatus, so that the objects of faith come to be seen not as metaphysical beings and forces but rather as religious postulates, guiding principles and goals. God will be seen as the personified religious ideal, indwelling us and guiding us. Faith will be internalized and moralized, so that instead of depending upon a world above us we will set out to attain a better world to come.

Secondly, in order to counter the egoism or eudaemonism which is so deeply engrained in our tradition, we need to cultivate an inner scepticism, non-attachment and disinterestedness by following something very like the traditional mystic's way of purgation. Such a spirituality is an appropriate response to our new perception of the status of man in the universe. It can free us both from our natural egoism and striving for power and from the desire to wield religious power over others, and so prepare us for an ethic of agapeistic value-creating love.

Thirdly, we have to come to see religious language as being not descriptive but expressive, action-guiding and symbolic.[6] Christian language is embedded in the Christian way of life, and gains its meaning from the manner in which it is used in the furtherance of that way of life. We should not fall into the intellectualist error of imagining that it has a meaning and a reference that can be grasped independently of the way of life that it prescribes.

In *Taking Leave of God* (1980) I tried to show that God can be demythologized into spirituality without religious loss, and so that an undogmatic and ascetical religious practice is possible within the context of the metaphysical agnosticism and anthropocentrism of modern culture. The most interesting criticisms came from those who felt that the book was too old-fashioned, too much caught up in the problems of the 1840s, the age of Feuerbach, Marx and Kierkegaard, too much under the strenuous influence of Kant, and so a book of law rather than of gospel, and in general too much of a half-way house. It represented a transitional rather than a final position, and incidentally I have since been amused to find its main theses wittily foreseen and demolished in Nietzsche's notebooks.[7]

So in the present essay I have gone a few steps further, to a somewhat more radical philosophical position. The earlier book was concerned mainly with God and spirituality; this one turns to the social side of religion, to ethics, redemption and the Kingdom of God. In doing so it emphasizes the revolutionary strain in Christianity. For today we have lost not only the old cosy sacred cosmology, but also the various forms of meliorist belief that for a time replaced it. With the disappearance of all objective encouragement and motives for ultimate optimism we confront a most alarming crisis. It is as if we face the end of the world and the coming of nihilism. Thus we now see that Friedrich Nietzsche, although a somewhat eccentric figure and also one who did a good deal to create his own unsavoury popular reputation, was a very shrewd prophet of our modern discontents. What he did not see so clearly was that Jesus' eschatological message about the dissolution of the existing social and religious order and the coming of the Kingdom of God has an unexpected prophetic relevance to the modern situation. It is as if the revolution he called for is one that we at last now face. When Antonio Gramsci said that we are in a time when the old order is dying and the new is not yet ready to be born, he was expressing the modern sense of living in the dark interim-time between two worlds; and Jesus had himself stood at that point, addressing his message to that condition and describing a new world which did not come then but which must come now if we are to survive.

In effect, the development of critical thinking and of the scientific outlook has now demythologized or demystified all the things that people have traditionally lived by. Religions, ideologies, moralities, and even such basic social institutions as marriage and the nation-state have all been reduced by sceptical analysis to complex cultural transforms and masks of the raw biological will to power. The sceptical biological naturalism of Machiavelli, Hobbes, Nietzsche and Freud has prevailed, and the realization of the extent to which human beings as we know them are ultimately motivated by egoistic will-to-power has coincided with our actual acquisition of destructive power on an almost unimaginable scale. A culture in any case driving towards nihilism now possesses the power of annihilation. There is no way of losing this power, and we are becoming accustomed to living on the edge of the abyss.

We have been brought to this pass by the fact that religion and culture hitherto have in the main been built upon and have tried to control, redirect and sublimate raw human nature. The Western tradition of independent critical and scientific thinking has simultaneously unmasked the various tricks that we have played upon ourselves to do this, and has created morally-blind and very powerful new knowledge-systems. Beneath the prosperous and humane surface of modern life there lurks a terribly-lucid madman with a grenade in his hand.

The Christian gospel declares that if we avail ourselves of the disciplines and practices of religion and are willing to pass through the fire of nihilism, it will burn out our natural egoism and bring us through on the far side to a new kind of human reality and a new basis for social life. I have no wish to conceal the arduousness of this spiritual journey. I did not undertake it willingly, and I only venture to recommend it now because we have come to a time when it is the only recourse left to us.

*   *   *

On a different note, some remarks about method may be helpful. Christian thought has always sought to come to terms with the dominant philosophy of the time, but in the great days of speculative metaphysics it was rather easier to grasp the issues than it is now. When philosophy and theology were both of them dogmatic you could set their respective maps of reality side by side and make a fairly direct comparison. By contrast, modern philosophy is critical and is concerned mainly with issues of knowledge, logic and language. It addresses itself to the deep structure of religious beliefs rather than to their manifest content. It is not particularly concerned to question or revise religious belief at the manifest level, and so it may seem, on the surface, to leave everything as it is. Philosophers themselves have no particular reason for becoming involved in either religious controversy or theological reconstruction, and the churches may not realize that current views in logic and the theory of knowledge have profound implications for our whole understanding of religious belief and practice. In recent years the philosophy of religion and radical theology have usually run on parallel tracks without touching each other. I have tried to make the connections by working out the implications for faith's own understanding of itself of at least some lines of thought in modern philosophy.

Religious thought has been changing very rapidly in recent years. For a long time theology addressed itself mainly to biblical criticism and issues raised by the history of Christian doctrine, but nowadays the rapid growth of religious studies has introduced new questions and new ways of thinking derived from less familiar sources; philosophy, the comparative study of religions, the social sciences, the history of ideas, anthropology, the psychology of religion and so on. The penetration of theology by these new influences is transforming consciousness and making older ways of thinking seem simply unintelligible. We are in another country now, with a new agenda. Sometimes it is suggested that the avant-garde religious thought of the 1960s was a brief aberration and that normality has since been restored, but the truth is rather the opposite. A profounder shift is already under way.

Many people worry about the implications of this shift for religious practice, but I suggest that the boot is on the other foot. It is those who are not making the shift who ought to be worried. Naive realism about the meaning of religious language generates a great supernatural apparatus which, in my experience, raises insoluble intellectual problems and which (in the rather psychologized form in which it has to be accepted nowadays) is deeply oppressive and mystifying. There is abundant evidence all around us that traditional theological realism is now an intellectual and psychological mess. By contrast, if you fully recognize the culturally-evolved and symbolic character of religious beliefs, and see that beyond all the imagery and beyond the limits of language there is only and *can* only be the deep peace and silence of the Ineffable, you are liberated. You are free to pursue the spirituality and the ethic and to practise the faith just for love's own sake, and its true claims become purer and clearer. What Professor Geach has rather disparagingly called 'the new undogmatic Christianity'[8] is so attractive and many people are taking to it so readily that I have felt compelled rather to emphasize the difficulties and to stress how hard it is (or should be), pointing out that it is a new and more demanding form of the old Christian way of *agnōsia* or unknowing.[9]

So I think in terms of gain rather than loss, but unfortunately in any change of this kind, word about the No gets around more quickly than word about the Yes. The No is quickly grasped; the Yes is strange to people who are strongly committed to other ways of thinking.

Finally, friends who are New Testament specialists sometimes charge me with making very selective use of the New Testament. I think there is an unavoidable difference here. The New Testament scholar's job is to give a full account of all that the New Testament writers meant in their time, whereas my concern is to seize only upon such elements and themes as can be put to creative use today. Any Christian writer will believe that there is some kind of analogy between Jesus and his own contemporary situation; but the record shows that the analogy is perceived differently in different periods, and that all such perceptions are and cannot but be highly selective.

Anyone who attempts to open up new lines of religious thought must expect a certain amount of aggravation, if he is a practising clergyman. I owe a debt of gratitude to those who have given me encouragement and support. To them I offer this essay.

1

HYPERBOREAN FAITH

According to Greek legend the Hyperboreans were a strange and out-of-the-way people who lived at the furthest extremity of the world, beyond Boreas the North Wind, beyond the ice, beyond death – and who had found in that seemingly insupportable region a land of warmth and plenty. Nietzsche refers to them when he says, 'Let us look one another in the face. We are Hyperboreans';[1] and now that some Hyperborean believers have appeared, it occurs to me that he was right: we do indeed need to look one another in the face and learn to recognize each other, for in these new and strange regions our eyes are confused and we have barely yet grasped where we are. The Church of the Hyperboreans remains invisible, its members largely unaware of each other and unconscious of themselves as a group, because we are still too preoccupied with memories of the lands we have left and the hard journey we have made to be able to grasp yet that we have after all come together in a place that – against all expectations – does turn out to be habitable.

The journey has taken us from an old world in which faith was experienced as a supernaturally prescribed and guided response to objective supernatural realities, to a new world in which faith is instead seen as a creative and freely-undertaken commitment to a life-path guided by rituals, myths, symbols and ideals; rituals, myths and so forth which, moreover, are fully and consciously acknowledged as such without even the most secret and residual attempt at self-deception. Having been deprived of the illusion that faith requires of us no more than assent to a picturesque ideology, we have begun to learn the hard way what it is actually to practise a religion just for its own sake.

Put like that, it does not sound too difficult a transition to make, and certainly it was forced upon us by the way theology had been developing for a long time. Since the late eighteenth century the Kantian critical philosophy had been bringing home to us the implications of the truism that human knowledge really is just human knowledge, a product of the constructive activity of the human mind; and the concept of myth, introduced into theology at about the same time, had been slowly working to persuade us that all human religious thinking is and can only be a thoroughly human and symbolic form of expression. Even more searching has been the effect of biblical criticism on the popular belief that we have in the Bible a special revelation of supernatural facts that are both genuinely historical and at the same time history-transcending, beyond criticism, and able to give theology a fixed foundation in the supernatural order. It now appears that all these supposed supernatural facts are human interpretative constructions, period pieces just as much immersed in the flux of history as we ourselves are. The idea of a primitive Golden Age somehow exempt from the ordinary limitations of human life and thought, in which norms that would govern all subsequent historical life were laid down, is now seen to be a rainbow's end which vanishes as one searches for it. The history of religions shows it to be no more than a standard mythological device for enforcing the social authority of a particular system of beliefs and values.

Thus theology has for two centuries been pushed steadily in the direction of historicism and anthropocentrism, a point of view that sees all human life and thought as immersed in the flow of history like a fish in a river. But traditional Christian thought had leaned heavily on authorities, absolutes, anchorage-points outside history. As all these anchorage-points gave way one after another, a sense of crisis developed. Reviewing the situation in 1972, David A. Pailin wrote:

> By the 1970s theology had probably reached the edge of either total collapse or a genuine reformation. All the old authorities – the Bible, the Church, the creeds, the councils, episcopacy and religious experience – were questioned. Having no established foundations or fixed norms, the theologian, possibly for

the first time in the Christian era, had the opportunity and was faced with the challenge to start again from the beginning.[2]

Six years later, in 1978, Professor John Kent came to an equally radical conclusion at the end of a detailed survey of the development of theology since the Enlightenment.[3] And the 'new beginning' of which Pailin speaks is, I suggest, the transition to Hyperborean faith.

But it is not at all an easy transition to make. To find faith again, or rather, to have to create it, on the far side of the loss of faith; to give up the old, protective surrounding framework of supernaturalist belief and move out into what at first seems to be a void – that is very hard. The task of creating *ex nihilo* did not sound too daunting so long as we imagined it to be solely the task of a god; at least, I never heard of anyone imagining that a god might be struck with sheer terror at the prospect of it. We never dreamt what it might involve, until we were confronted with it ourselves.

In reaching (or at least, approaching) a position which was metaphysically agnostic, radically anthropocentric, and dominated by a kind of linguistic naturalism and historicism, theology showed that it is inescapably subject to the same intellectual forces that are at work elsewhere in the culture. Many people deplore this, arguing that in their thinking theologians should be guided by completely autonomous principles of method, and should obstinately stay in precisely the same place by swimming always against the stream. But the demand that is being made here is in fact confused, for it presumes that there can be timeless thinking and language. Such a thing may perhaps be possible in preliterate cultures, but at any rate once writing and history have appeared it is obvious that every piece of discourse is datable, *whatever* its topic or its degree of originality. We cannot even imagine what an entirely dateless intellectual method or literary text or piece of discourse could be like. The implications of this realization have been spelt out in recent years by the French historian of systems of thought, Michel Foucault. He takes diverse subjects such as biology, linguistics and economics, and shows a common intellectual framework underlying the way they were pursued in the Age of Reason; and he then shows them as undergoing closely analogous transformations as the modern period arrives at the end of the eighteenth century.[4] Whatever the subject, in any given period certain ways of thinking are available, and others are not available. To quote a case not mentioned by Foucault, the early biblical scholars had already, in the manner of Linnaeus, described and classified biblical manuscripts, noting their divergences from the Received Text; but then in the nineteenth century the critics began to group the manuscripts into families, to work out their genealogical relationships and to construct theories of the evolution of the text. In short, they were doing just the same thing in their field as Darwin was to do in biology. Formally, Darwin's argument in the *Origin of Species* that the ready classifiability of species into genera and families is *prima facie* evidence of their common descent[5] was exactly the same argument as that used by the textual critics. It was a style of argument which the culture of the period made available to thinkers, in whatever field they were working. Given that there is in a certain period a community of scholars engaged in debate and together seeking understanding, we can scarcely imagine them not making use of the culturally available tools of understanding; a principle which applies just as much to theologians as to anyone else.

So there is no escape from history and language. Language is wholly human and social, and all linguistic meanings are human social products. Everywhere in its use, language inevitably embodies a human point of view. Man is the only maker of meaning: that is, human beings, in their ceaseless struggle to impose life-sustaining patterns of meaning and order upon the flux of experience, continually generate fictions to live by; but all these life-guiding patterns of meaning, both the less successful and the more, are social constructions and as such are subject to continual historical change. No facts are perceptible except through the spectacles of some theory or other; but no historical perspective or scientific theory dare claim nowadays to be more than the product of a provisional and temporary consensus. For the present, it seems to help us to find our way about the world and to make a sort of sense of experience, but as it recently superseded another pattern, so it is itself presumably subject to eventual replacement in its turn. When the growth of knowledge and the pace of change are so rapid that we are conscious even within our own lifetime of having lived through revolutionary changes of perspective in all branches of knowledge and in morality and religion, then it is brought home to us that in the modern period all absolutes have dissolved – including even consciousness and personal identity, for the spectator himself changes as what he sees changes. Shall we say that there is only human creativity and the flux? No, not even that, for neither the creativity nor the flux can be perceived 'pure', but the former only in its action and the latter only in its various constructions.

Hume, the patron of modern English-language philosophy, had arrived at something like this position in the eighteenth century: scepticism, naturalism and anthropocentrism. Wittgenstein in our own century modifies Hume's position and partly overcomes his scepticism by emphasizing the public character of language. Language already presupposes a society of language-users, and has a commonly-arrived-at conception of the world built into it. Thus Wittgenstein's linguistic naturalism emphasizes the social character of human creativity. By contrast, Nietzsche disparaged social creativity, and instead assigned the highest value to the creative power of the exceptional individual who coins new metaphors and opens up new life-possibilities. But he thought that by the time they have been assimilated into the common language these new metaphors have lost their power. For him, the moment of first creation is all.[6] So it is no accident that Nietzsche's first great influence was upon the modern movement in art in the early part of this century, whereas Anglo-Saxon philosophy has concerned itself rather with the more obviously communal enterprise of natural science. In other respects, though, gaps are closing. Nietzsche has come to be seen as the patron of modern continental philosophy, the resemblance of his philosophy to Hume's has been pointed out,[7] and interest in his thought has become strong in the English-speaking world. Concern for language and the genealogy of ways of thinking, radical anthropocentrism and constructivism in the theory of knowledge – here is common ground.

This newly emerging common ground is not the same as the 'liberalism' or the 'secularism' which were diagnosed by theology in recent generations. It may be historicist, but that does not imply any revival of the belief in progress; it may be anthropocentric, but it does not presuppose any special confidence in human goodness or perfectibility, nor even any standard conception of human nature (on the contrary, Nietzsche insists that 'man must be overcome', and Foucault that 'the death of man' has already occurred); and it may be naturalistic, but not in the sense that we have a stable and assured picture of what the world or 'reality' is: far from it.

Thus the challenge to theology is to come to terms not with liberalism or secularism, but with a newer and rather different constellation of ideas, far more fluid and subversive. Not only 'the death of God' has occurred, but the death of 'the cosmos' and of man. We are uncertain of our ability to fix clear, objective and truly enduring conceptions of *anything*. All is flux and multifariousness, with recurrent attempts individual and communal to establish patterns of meaning that will hold for a while; but the frame hold keeps collapsing and one has to return to twiddling with the knobs to re-establish some sort of readable and usable picture. Paradoxically, with the spectacular growth of modern knowledge there has come also an alarming recognition of its historically-conditioned, transitory and merely human character:

> What then is truth? A mobile army of metaphors, metonymies, anthropomorphisms; a sum, in short, of human relationships which, rhetorically and poetically intensified, ornamented and transformed, come to be thought of, after long usage by a people, as fixed, binding and canonical. Truths are illusions which we have forgotten are illusions, worn-out metaphors now impotent to stir the senses, coins which have lost their faces and are considered now as metal rather than currency.[8]

The world really is in continual change; all ideas of fixed and unalterable frameworks are gone, and knowledge and morality have to be continually reminted. Today's liberating new metaphor will by tomorrow have lapsed into a leaden cliché, a prison that must be escaped from. We have to create to live.

Hyperborean faith represents an attempt to live a free and truthful Christian life, without nostalgia, illusion or the traditional insatiable hunger for power over others, in the world as it now is. That is a great deal to ask, for it involves a most painful shift from traditional attitudes and few will be prepared to make it; but some outlines of what it requires can now be discerned.

It will be so *un*theological that I hesitate even to use the expression 'radical theology' to describe it. Traditional theology had the grandiose ambition, suggested by the form of the creeds, of giving a kind of sketch of ultimate reality and an outline history of the cosmos from beginning to end. Today such ambition seems absurd. We will have to be content to argue that a certain spirituality and form of life are possible, desirable and liberating, and to show what is involved. Besides, it is notorious that theology in the past was obsessively preoccupied with questions of authority, power and control. The first theologians of all, in early Egypt and Mesopotamia, were concerned to arrange the different gods and sanctuaries in orderly hierarchies of power and control; and the first Christian theologian, St Paul, was eager to show the implications of his doctrine for the authority of church leaders over congregations, men over women, parents over children, and masters over servants. The subsequent waxing of the church's social power and its increasingly exalted and exclusive doctrinal claims were two sides of the same coin, for the church's sole possession of ultimately-important truth was the same thing as its authority to control the commanding heights of the culture. In later times, as the church deepened its control over the moral and emotional life of the laity, the confessor's manual of moral theology equipped him to interrogate and search the soul of his penitent, teaching the penitent to see himself inwardly as the church wanted him to see himself. Because 'knowledge works as a tool of power',[9] we readily detect 'empire-building' in every rising professional or academic group that develops a special body of knowledge; and when we apply metaphors drawn from religion to describe the behaviour of such a group – the way it maintains orthodoxy, initiates disciples, cultivates a mystique, defends its prerogatives, establishes exclusive claims and so forth – we acknowledge that religion was the original example of the principle. Nor was Protestant internalization a satisfactory solution to the problem of religious power, for it turned the terrible power of religious doctrine inward against the self, as we are reminded by Chillingworth's old saying that 'Luther had a Pope in his belly'.[10] Here was but a new form of the old bargain: Accept absolute domination over your inmost self, and you will find that in and through that acceptance you will be given a like power over others. That will be your reward; and that is true religion, a chain of inner bondage.

Well, a really thorough critique of religious power has never yet been carried out, but it is evident today that we have to free ourselves from the last vestiges of any desire to make such a bargain. Indeed, I suspect that there was always an obscure perception that in making that horrible bargain one was not saving one's soul but selling it. Nevertheless, much of theology as we have received it was an elaborate justification for the making of that bargain. And if today we can reach the point where we have no wish at all either to be dominated or to dominate, then the chain breaks, and much of the traditional sort of theology is no longer required. Symbols and practices from the tradition will be used, so far as they are helpful, as guides to the spiritual life, but the main emphasis will be on freedom, creativity and spiritual mobility. God will be seen not as 'king of kings' and apex of the cosmic power-pyramid but as Spirit, indeterminable, an inner principle of freedom, the guiding ideal and goal of the spiritual life. Destructive and alienating images of God, as one who legitimates the exercise of power over others or who fixates us in a condition of inner alienation, will fall away. Faith will free itself from the old yearning to fall under the domination of illusions that it has itself projected and then use them to dominate others in turn: it will be intellectually cleansed.

In some circles in the USA a religious position called 'fictionalism' is discussed. The idea is that in the modern period we have come to realize that myths are myths and we have now to reconcile myth and consciousness, the continuing utilization of religious mythology with our modern realization of its true character. It is argued that the irrational is a very large part of human nature, that the conscious element in the self rests on dark and murderous instincts like a man clutching on to the back of a tiger in dreaming,[11] and that only symbol, myth and ritual have the power to handle that tiger. Because the irrational has so large a part in us, it is, if you like, 'rational' to make use of seemingly irrational beliefs which are able (in a way we cannot fully understand) to tame it. Besides, the world itself is not rational; it is only *made* so by our ceaseless struggle to impose patterns of order upon it, and these patterns are themselves human fictions. Whether we are speaking of the use of scientific and technological fictions to order the world around us, or of the use of religious fictions to gain self-knowledge, self-mastery and freedom, the question is only, Which fictions work best? The test of truth can in the end only be pragmatic. So in today's all-pervading uncertainties Christian intellectuals, for the present at least, must learn to live with a fictionalist view of their own faith.

Such a view has some similarity to the one I am describing, and it represents an advance on fideism, its historical predecessor. In the sixteenth and seventeenth centuries many thinkers were troubled by the seeming impossibility of finding a genuinely independent touchstone of religious truth.[12] Religious doctrines, it seemed, could neither be proved nor disproved by reason, so that one might equally well believe or disbelieve. But why not in that case simply suspend belief? It certainly looks as if many fideists decided that in a society where certain beliefs and practices are customary, and indeed enforced by authority with formidable sanctions, the prudent sceptic should conform, professing himself a believer by faith alone in matters which reason is not competent to resolve. But such an attitude merely postpones challenging an authority grown old and tyrannical, and has an air of timorousness about it. It could be used to justify laziness in the struggle for freedom.

Fictionalism is a degree or two bolder than fideism, but I am still a little suspicious of it. Radical at the level of philosophy, but conservative at the level of theology and religious practice, it can easily appear to be yet another device for maintaining the status quo with the minimum of aggravation. The old faith is represented as coexisting alongside the modern consciousness of its true character; and apparently there is little need for revision. Only a small minority of the congregation will be able to articulate the modern awareness of the true character of religious beliefs, and if they are prudent and talk to each other in a private academic code they will not disturb the rest at all. It is rather as if a few of those enthusiastically taking part in the tribal ceremonies are visiting anthropologists in disguise. Later on, after they have jetted back to their campuses in the West, they will debate the theory of ritual among themselves; but meanwhile they take part in the ceremonies in good faith and certainly love and admire the culture they are sharing. But this situation cannot last: though the anthropologists might wish to see the tribal culture preserved intact and therefore try to keep the two levels of thought and practice separate, the fact is that Westernization is coming and the tribal culture will be wiped out by it. No doubt the anthropologists are doing a worthwhile job, and a scientist does not want to interfere with the

phenomena he is studying, but there is also a place for someone
who will stand alongside the tribesmen and try to help them carry
something of their traditional faith and values through the approaching crisis of Westernization. A purely descriptive philosophy of religion may be content to behave like the visiting
anthropologists, but a philosopher of religion who is also a
churchman will prefer the second role. He is like a tribesman who
has had a Western education. He knows what is coming, and he
experiences the conflict of the cultures within himself. To him, the
view that the tribal beliefs and ceremonies can be conserved
simply as socially-valuable fictions is only a temporary solution.
In the longer term something more radical is needed.

So the believer I am describing feels he must go a stage beyond
fictionalism, and attempt to be really truthful about where we are
now and what we are now. The modern consciousness is or seeks
to be free, self-aware and entirely undogmatic, and it fully accepts
its own fluidity, mobility and impermanence. Its joy is in self-
realization through creative self-expression. In what form can
Christian faith come through to such a person? It has to be, by
completing the internalization of Christianity. As the New Testament puts it, there has to be a movement forward from milk to
meat, from the letter to the Spirit, from the religion of a schoolboy
under authority to that of an adult who decides for himself.[13] We
are still under the spell of the old objectified religion of the slave
societies of antiquity and the feudal societies of the Middle Ages,
which projected religious realities out as a many-tiered hierarchy
of authorities above man and as an ornate supernaturalist cosmology. But there was already in the Bible a promise of liberation
by internalization, and the modern movement towards it began
with Eckhart and others who lived in the towns along the Rhine
in the later medieval period. Luther, Pascal, Kierkegaard and
others continued the process, and the task is now to complete it.
Faith will become a free decision to follow the Christian path to
holiness because it is recognized that the highest form of creative
self-realization is, paradoxically, that of which selflessness makes
us capable, and because it is seen that the practice of disinterested
love is the highest basis for society and the best response to our
mortality.

To float above seventy thousand fathoms, far from all human
aid, and yet be glad — how is that possible? Only by a religious

discipline. But the ascetical disciplines of the past can no more be
adopted uncritically than its doctrines, which after all they reflect.
Sometimes doctrine portrayed a God who was a strange mixture
of cruelty and love, who had created suffering human beings in
order himself to suffer inexpressibly and yet joyfully in contemplating and in sharing their sufferings; and the ascetic could only
too easily follow suit, treating his own alienated bodily nature as
God seemed to treat the world, suffering with a fierce satisfaction
in contemplating his own self-mortification. His life taught one
great message – that punishment is the creator of consciousness.
Seeing something godlike in this, many cultures in the past revered
advanced ascetics and credited them with supernatural powers,
but today there has been a widespread revulsion against the
excesses of the traditional intropunitive psychology. Recoiling
from them, people are also rejecting the associated images of God,
with implications more radical than they yet realize. But Christian
spirituality still needs an inner discipline. If it is to make faith,
make love, make gladness above seventy thousand fathoms, then
it must find new ways to do it. God's will for us must coincide
with our will to freedom, God's victory over sin must be our
abandonment of the old perverse religious psychology, and the
test of the presence of divine love in us must be how generously
and disinterestedly we will the *other*'s freedom with our own.

Here is a glimpse of the religious solution to the problem of
power. Dostoyevsky had portrayed his Christ-figures, Sonia,
Myshkin and Alyosha, as powerless and incapable of retaliation,
so given over to ecstatic other-centred love as to seem weak in the
head. Not having enough ego to stand up for themselves, they
were nothing but naked vulnerable love. Biologically, they seem
very implausible beings, but there is no doubt that the type has a
strong influence in our tradition. For many ordinary people it
represents the Christian ideal, and it arouses in them an odd
mixture of respect, reluctant fascination . . . and disgust. Studying
Dostoyevsky in 1887–8, Nietzsche reacted in just that way,
accepting 'the idiot' as the original and highest Christian ideal
and describing Christianity as nihilistic. He then flew to the
opposite extreme in his strongly biological ethic of strife and the
will to power, and so presented us with a disagreeable choice. He
had rejected the twisted ecclesiastical use of power that he traced
to late ancient Judaism and St Paul, and that left only a choice

between Jesus' complete withdrawal from power, and an unin-
hibited and cruel affirmation of the will to power. Perhaps
Nietzsche excluded too quickly the possibility of an intermediate
solution to the problem of power. The task is to learn to say Yes
to life, and to find the highest fulfilment of our capacity for
freedom, creativity and joy in life; and a hard inner discipline will
be needed. But the choice of a discipline is not a solitary choice, by
and for oneself, between a way of world-negating powerlessness
and a way of aggressive world-affirmation and self-affirmation. I
have argued elsewhere[14] that when the idea of God is fully
internalized in each of us it acts as a religious ideal that is both
inward and universal, pointing us to a way of fulfilment through
disinterestedness. To obtain my own highest fulfilment I have to
learn consistently to will that of others, for the path to oneself
goes through others and their freedom is ours. A theology of
liberation must be a social theology.

Finally, the Hyperborean faith of which I have been giving a
preliminary sketch does not by any means exclude the mystical. It
certainly refuses illusions and false consolation, but there are
many examples in the history of philosophy which show that a
rigorous and sceptical temper of mind, far from excluding,
actually purifies the sense of the mystical. Among modern examples one might mention Fritz Mauthner (1849–1923) and Wittgenstein. The latter's views are well-known: as for Mauthner, he
is an interesting pioneer of ordinary-language philosophy.[15] The
ability to think is for him identical with the ability to produce
language, and language is through-and-through human; there
cannot be any way of transcending language in order to see the
world from an absolute and extra-human point of view. Language
orders the world at three different levels: at the adjectival level the
world is pointillistic, phenomenal, a field of distinct qualities; at
the verbal level it is seen in terms of activity, event and process;
and at the nominal level it is seen as a world of things or objects.
But these are all levels of linguistic construction, and the philosophy of language, in pointing this out, is itself in no way exempt
from the inescapable limits of language. So Mauthner's critique
of language led him to radical anthropocentrism or, as he called
it, 'hominism'; but he also insisted that 'critique of language is the
road to mysticism'. The more strictly you insist upon the limits of
the sayable, the more vividly you are aware of the vastness and

purity of the Ineffable. But since this mysticism is awakened precisely by a strict insistence on the limits of language, it must remain non-cognitive. To go on sentimentally to objectify and personify the Ineffable would be an unpardonable weakness and inconsistency. The Ineffable cannot be invoked to *explain* anything, and though Mauthner pays tribute to the power of religious language as poetry and as a vehicle for expressing religious sentiments, he obviously cannot for a moment regard it as descriptively true. Thus he states very well and clearly the reasons why in our cultural situation the stringent intellectual purity of the Negative Way is the best way to maintain a truly religious spirit; and of course those who do not claim any privileged gnosis of the Ineffable are humble and do not wish to wield religious power over others. That Mauthner called himself an 'atheist' and his mysticism 'godless' is unimportant to any but the Boeotians He himself was deeply indebted to Eckhart.

Yet there are plenty of Boeotians about these days, and for the life of them they cannot see what motivates someone who takes serious exception to their point of view. What is all the fuss about? Here is an example, taken from recent events: the day after the Pope was shot in May 1981 the London *Times* carried a number of items relating to the ideas of prayer and providence. A facetious correspondence about prayers for victory in sporting contests was continuing, on the basis of an agreed but unvoiced ironical attitude to the efficacy of intercession; while elsewhere in the same issue many reports told how the millions were being exhorted to pray for the Pope and flocking to special Masses. Meanwhile the Pope was actually being treated not by religious rituals but with all the best resources of secular scientific medicine, and the doctors were loyally playing the game by declaring that a special intervention of Providence had deflected the bullet and caused it to miss the spinal column.

Now it is no doubt the case that most people see nothing incongruous in all this, and no doubt for a long time to come church leaders will continue to be compelled to endorse it by public opinion and by the media, which nowadays so largely prescribe what may and may not be said for public consumption. But there are a few people to whom it is a matter of deep concern that a once great religious tradition should, through sheer laziness and sentimentality, have allowed itself to decline into such a farrago of rather-less-than-half-believed superstition, and it is for them only that I write. If you are one of them, you may like to join me in search of the faith of the age to come.

2

RELIGIOUS CHANGE AND THE POLITICS OF TRUTH

Because the sacred and all that surrounds it always seems to be ancient and inviolable, the very idea of modernizing or reformulating religious belief is repugnant to many people. They detect an impious and question-begging assumption that religion is man-made and may be refashioned to suit our own whims. Such refashioning certainly happens, as when modern feminists set about updating the image of God, but to the conservative believer and his old ally the right-wing satirist it seems an obvious absurdity. They regard it as axiomatic that religious beliefs are timeless truths, proof against historical change.

Yet in fact all religious beliefs have histories behind them. They were formulated by people who lived at certain times in the past in certain social situations and conducted certain controversies. From the historian's point of view *every* religious position is a human historical product, and the history of religions is a history of continual change. How could it be otherwise?

The two points of view are perhaps not necessarily incompatible, for it might be that a particular religious doctrine was indeed formulated at a particular place and time in history as a result of violent controversy, and bearing all the marks of its period of origin and so forth – and yet is simply true, in the strongest and most philosophical sense. Many Roman Catholics presumably think this. But there is the further point that meanings are not historically constant. Religious beliefs during their historical transmission prove to be highly elastic, being interpreted and put to use in quite different ways as they are taken up into and function

as parts of successive different cultural totalities. Held in a
particular period, a belief is dyed through and through with the
characteristic colour of that period, and no part of it remains
untinged. Thus the history of religion is a history of great
meaning-shifts, as the received tradition repeatedly gets shaken
up and falls into a quite new pattern. And I believe such a
meaning-shift is occurring today.

An indication of its nature is given in the first sentence of John
Wisdom's pioneering essay, 'Gods' (1944)[1]: 'The existence of God
is not an experimental issue in the way it was.' Wisdom went on
to cite Elijah's contest with the prophets of Baal on Mount Carmel,
by way of making the point that whereas Elijah had arranged a
kind of experimental test to find out whose god was more
powerful, we could scarcely imagine our own religious leaders
doing the same thing nowadays. Religious belief is apparently no
longer that kind of thing. Wisdom went on to suggest that religious
beliefs do not convey extra facts to us, but rather affect the way
we see all the facts. Belief in God had once been a factual
hypothesis, a claim that all events are controlled by an invisible
person behind the scenes; but today it seems that belief in God has
become a perspectival rather than a factual question. Believing in
God is a way of interpreting experience that brings out certain
depths of meaning in life, and makes certain valuable experiences
possible. What is more, disputes about how to see the facts,
though not themselves factual, are often nonetheless real disputes
on which a great deal may hang.

It is noticeable that although Wisdom rejected literal theism, he
did not move over to an existentialist or purely practical interpretation of religious language, but instead continued to worry about
the cognitive side of religious belief and experience. Yet twenty-
five years later he was still unable to formulate a view that satisfied
him.[2]

The more radical implications of Wisdom's paper were not
followed up immediately. For a while, the issues continued to be
debated according to the rules laid down by the positivists. If
religious beliefs were meaningful then they must incorporate
factual claims; and if so, then it must be possible to specify some
turn of events that could show them to be untrue. So *could*
religious beliefs be falsified by experience, and what d tectable
difference did it make whether they were true or not? This was

really a pre-Wisdom way of seeing the issues, for it regarded religious beliefs as being more-or-less factual hypotheses; nevertheless, at least some believers were willing to play the game according to the positivist rules. They did their best – not very successfully, it must be admitted – to show how the facts of life could tell for and against religious claims.[3]

However, as the influence of positivism declined, it became clearer that the positivist way of setting up the issues had been a mistake. Philosophy of religion on these terms was a dead end. So a few bolder spirits rejected the common assumption that religious beliefs purport to describe supernatural facts and instead put forward what were then called 'non-cognitive' theories of religious belief. R. M. Hare[4] and, more recently, Norman Malcolm[5] have argued that religious beliefs are among those groundless and ultimate beliefs which express one's fundamental slant on life. R. B. Braithwaite[6] and T. R. Miles[7] moved towards ethics in presenting versions of the view that to be a religious believer is to be committed to a certain way of life illustrated by a set of stories, myths or parables. Braithwaite has unfortunately written no more on the philosophy of religion, but Miles, who is a Quaker, added an interesting little book which defends a non-cognitive view of religious experience.[8] In this book he aligns himself with Bishop John Robinson, and so makes one of the few connections between the philosophy of religion and the concurrent debates among theologians about secularization, radical theology and the death of God. In fact the philosophers and the theologians were talking about the same issues, but in very different idioms. Hare, for example, says:

The more primitive a religion is, the more readily are its statements open to empirical falsification; religion has advanced from its more primitive to its less primitive forms partly by the empirical falsification of the more primitive forms, which then come to be known as superstitions. . . . Thus the prescriptive, attitudinal element in religion gains at the expense of the descriptive, factual element.[9]

Here is a return to the radical theme in John Wisdom's paper, and it clearly resembles Robinson's shift from literal to metaphorical theism, and my own recent attempt to go all the way in the same direction.

Hare's hint that the factual elements in religious belief come in time to be seen as superstitions has been taken up and developed most forcibly by D. Z. Phillips.[10] Phillips has been a good deal criticized in philosophical circles, and his name is not well known in the churches, but he is probably the most interesting and original British religious thinker of the post-war period. He took up Wittgenstein's idea of 'language-games' and argued that religious language is an autonomous and distinctive way of speaking with its own internal criteria of truth and meaningfulness. We can show how it works, but there is no sense in the idea that one might be able to step outside the limits of religious language and check its accuracy by comparing the religious representation of God with the original. Phillips thinks that the assumption behind such an ambition is mistaken, and he consistently describes theological realism – any suggestion that religious beliefs describe supernatural facts, or that religious acts are causally efficacious – as superstition. True religion is attitudinal, expressive, symbolic, and it stays within the limits of language. Phillips' position is so strict that it leaves him little latitude for discussing and explaining religious change or the diversity of religions. He simply states his view as to the form true religion must take today, and that view is clearly metaphysically agnostic. Theologians have been intrigued by the light he sheds on theologies such as that of Karl Barth, and still more by the fact that the non-realist Phillips shows an understanding of the movement of religious ideas much better than that of his realist critics. Alone among modern writers, he actually makes one think that an account of Christianity which is not based on belief that there is a metaphysical God out there might be religiously superior to the usual account.

This returns us to John Wisdom's opening sentence. For it is plain that over a very long period now religious belief has indeed been gradually abandoning its old explanatory and descriptive pretensions. Until the eighteenth century it was normal for disasters such as fire, pestilence, earthquake and shipwreck to be interpreted theologically, and a case like the firing of Old St Paul's in London by lightning on 4 June 1561 shows how very important it was to the authorities that the correct theological interpretation of the event should become fixed in the minds of the people. The fire had taken place on the eve of Corpus Christi, and to some it was a warning of divine displeasure at the government's Protestant policy, whereas to others it was a sign that the process of reform should be speeded up.[11] Throughout Elizabeth's reign there was a steady stream of official theological interpretations of unsettling events. In the case of the earthquake of 6 April 1580 it was declared that although earthquakes might sometimes be caused naturally, this particular one was the outcome of a special divine intervention to warn people against immodest dress, neglect of the Sabbath, and other sins against the social order.[12]

It was only very gradually that such ways of interpreting events became less important to governments and churchmen, but in the celebrated test case of the Lisbon earthquake of All Saints' Day 1755 the voices arguing that all theological explanations, whether Catholic, Protestant or deist, were equally inappropriate had become appreciably stronger.[13] Victorian preachers still delivered admonitory sermons on railway accidents, shipwrecks and the like,[14] but there is an air of jest in the comments about the thunderstorm which accompanied the proclamation of papal infallibility in 1870. Today it would seem very odd to interpret a major air crash as an act of divine judgment, and the great earthquake of 23 November 1980 in Southern Italy was seen less as a problem in speculative religious thought than as a call to practical religious action.

Now how are we to interpret this religious change? In Elizabeth I's time the prevailing concept of God was strongly realist and interventionist. Then, as the idea of the universal reign of physical law became stronger, many came to hold a view of God which, though still realist, was increasingly non-interventionist. In addition, as human ability to understand and control nature grew, there was a desire to distance God from responsibility for disasters which, it was felt, should rather be blamed on human negligence, lack of foresight, and the faulty design or operation of machines or bridges. It was increasingly felt that human sinfulness, rather than God, was to be blamed for the terrible sufferings of men in war.

In this development the secularist, who cannot see the movement of religious thought from within and can only understand an objectified and realist view of God, naturally perceives a steady loss of explanatory power and fading away of God. In parallel with the earthly sovereign, God declines from the active and potent absolute monarch of Elizabethan times to the well-loved and gracious but ineffectual and merely symbolic monarch of modern times. Real power has shifted elsewhere. However, if the secularist view of God as being no more than an outmoded explanatory hypothesis were correct, it would be difficult to understand why religion survives and is so strong as it is today, in a time when God has no explanatory value left whatever and plays no constitutive role in the theoretical scheme of any major branch of knowledge.

A more plausible explanation, then, is that religion is not disappearing but is changing in the way indicated by Richard Hare in the passage quoted above. The old realist and interventionist idea of God has now become a superstition. The intellectual difficulty that the churches find themselves in is the political impossibility of their openly admitting to themselves the vast change that is taking place in their real, as opposed to their ostensible, beliefs.

For the fact is that today we are far less inclined to discuss and compare religions in terms of the descriptive truth of their dogmas. Instead we commonly assess a religion as a whole way of life, asking about its symbol-system, its rites, its ethic, its spirituality and the kind of person it tends to produce. We are less interested in religion as a speculative theory of the world – so far as that is concerned, natural science is the best we have got, and all that we have got – and we prefer instead to regard religion as a maker of community and as a source of inspiration and values to live by. When I hear preachers testifying to the power of the gospel of God's love revealed in Christ and extolling the power of this gospel to conquer evil and suffering, I notice that they do not nowadays find it necessary even to discuss the objection, obvious from the realist point of view, that the very same love whose power over evil they extol has itself with infinite care selected for infliction upon us every last detail of the evils and injustices we face. People are evidently much less inclined now to think of God as personally ordaining all the sorrows that afflict humanity, though if they were still realists, as they pretend to be, they should. But the truth is that, *de facto* if not yet *de jure*, God now functions in religious language principally as a symbol of the authority of religious values and claims. God is love. The power of God is the power of love, and moral commitment to God is moral commitment to the way of love. I appeal to the facts of usage: listen to what people say and you will find that that is what, on the whole, they now mean, although they do not admit it. What I have somewhat romantically described as Hyperborean faith is an attempt to become fully conscious of what religious language as used today now really means, whatever people's professions to the contrary. I know they will deny it, but that is for 'political' reasons; in practice religious concepts are increasingly used in an attitudinal and prescriptive way and no longer in an explanatory and descriptive way. For example, doctrines are invoked nowadays not because they are simply and factually true as such, but by way of enforcing a point in social ethics.

So we have come to make a rather sharp distinction between the provinces of science and religion. Neither gives us absolute truth. Science *explains* phenomena in nature by showing how they are regularly related to other phenomena in nature, and its goal is in the end to define all these regular patterns in the language of mathematics. Religion *reconciles* us to the facts of life by giving them concentrated symbolic expression. Thus far, it is like art; but it goes beyond art in that its way of symbolizing is community-building, liberating and life-guiding. It offers something like an artistic vision of the world – which also prescribes a way of life.

Evidently there is a dual problem here: there is the task of defining the religious change that is taking place, and there is the further question of whether the churches can become fully conscious of its true character, or must slide ever further into self-deception and illusion. The change is taking place, for everybody; but one has only reached Hyperborean faith when one has become fully conscious of it within oneself. It is remarkably easy to make the change and deny that you have made it, but surprisingly difficult to become fully and openly conscious of it.

The difficulty arises because for the churches truth is so strongly political, so much a matter of group-feeling and loyalty to the community and its traditions. Theological views are always assessed in purely political terms, so that every theologian is categorized as being conservative, liberal or radical, as responsible or irresponsible, as moderate or extremist, sound or unsound, reliable or unreliable, judicious or injudicious; and matters are so arranged that those who attempt to raise consciousness find themselves stigmatized, pushed to the margins and made ineffective. Those who wish to maintain unconsciousness are always firmly entrenched at the centre, and are able to protect their position by political labelling of anything that threatens them. It is as if the conservatives themselves half-realize that 'orthodoxy' is nowadays not a matter of descriptive truth but of political solidarity, and 'heresy' is not error but dissent.

No single word illustrates the problem more clearly than the word 'myth', which is always introduced as a consciousness-raising tool and always provokes the same sharp reaction. From about the 1920s to the early 1960s the dominant movement within Christian thought was neo-orthodoxy, a sort of sophisticated fundamentalism which strongly emphasized biblical categories of thought, revelation, dogma and the uniqueness of Christianity. The chief ideological tool used in resisting the raising of consciousness was the doctrine of revelation, used to justify a very sharp division between Christianity and other religions. Christianity was God's gift to man, but all other faiths were just mythological expressions of human religiosity, and could be sufficiently described by history, the social sciences and the psychology of religion. Thus neo-orthodoxy was able to fend off unwelcome questions for several decades by projecting them all on to other faiths and asking none of them of itself, a classic diversionary tactic.

By about 1960 biblical theology had broken down, partly because of internal developments within theology, and partly through external pressures. Theologians saw that it was too unphilosophical and so was incapable of contributing to the very important debate with philosophy which we have mentioned. Meanwhile, European cultural domination of the world was being questioned, many countries were becoming multi-faith or pluralistic societies, and official missionary policy changed from simple conversion to dialogue. The comparative study of religions expanded as an academic subject at every level. It became impossible to maintain a very sharp distinction between ways of thinking appropriate within Christian theology and ways of thinking appropriate when talking about other faiths. It was noticed that the ideological devices by which Christianity had sought to protect its own sense of a privileged status were paralleled by similar devices in other traditions; and to become aware of these devices as such was to relativize them, to realize that they are indeed just political devices and no more than that.

Again, the study of religions brings home to us the immense diversity of religious belief-systems, their historical mutability and their close relation to particular phases of social and cultural development. It may show that religion in one form or another is universal, but it also forces us to recognize how deeply embedded it is in history and human nature. Contemplating all this variety, we can hardly avoid the thought that in religion we deal, not with straightforward true-or-false descriptions of supernatural beings, but with ever-changing and historically-conditioned symbolic expressions of human spirituality; that is, with myth. If we wish to claim that the many-sided religious life of mankind bears witness to a transcendent reality, we will also have to admit that there are no non-symbolic statements about that Transcendent. How could there be? So far as we are concerned it can only be a bare and ineffable point, an imaginary focus of aspiration.

In 1973 John Hick announced his adherence to a position that might be called multifaith monotheism.[15] Instead of seeing our own religion as being at the centre of the universe, we should think of all the great world religions as circling round God as the planets orbit the sun. This was a valuable attempt to escape from the political limitations of previous Christian theologies, but the analogy it rests on is somewhat misleading. The planets are all rather similar bodies, we know they orbit around a common focus, and the sun around which they orbit is a body that is *independently* visible and describable. In the case of religion none of these points holds. The religions are very different from each other. Each is a highly complex symbol-system. It is by no means clear that they all point towards and converge upon a common focus, and we have no independent knowledge of or way of speaking about that which is supposed to be their common focus. We have many myths and symbols and we have ways of describing and explaining their use in particular traditions, but we have no independent access to the thing symbolized. Thus the study of religions today seems to be pulling its leading practitioners in the direction of a view of religion that is anthropocentric and mythical or symbolist.

By the late 1970s, around the time when *The Myth of God Incarnate*[16] was published, it was possible to say something like

this: 'We must now learn to live with the interplay between myth
and criticism, enchantment and consciousness. Historical criticism has made us aware, for example, of the process by which the
figure of Jesus came to be clothed with certain mythic vestments
drawn from the thought-world of Graeco-Roman antiquity. How
could it have been otherwise? They could only express his sacred
significance for them in the vocabulary available to them. Nor can
we strip off all the mythology and find the real, non-mythical
religious meaning of Jesus underneath. There is no non-mythical
religious meaning. There has to be myth, and there is only myth.
Today we must accept the human and mythical character of
religious belief even while at the same time, by meditating on it,
learning its logic and exploring it, we strive to rediscover its
redemptive and consoling power. For various reasons we have
been too disparaging about myth in the past. We now need
something like the interpretative skills of a literary critic to bring
out its meaning. After all, it is possible for a critic to analyse a
work of art and show us how it works as art, without by his
activity weakening its power as art. Similarly, a new religious
hermeneutics is needed to replace the old dogmatic theology. We
have to learn how religion can become fully conscious of its own
logic while yet remaining effective as religion.' [17]

In this way recent debate has suggested that the old realist
dogmatic theology may be replaced by a new religious hermeneutics. But the old dogmatics had performed certain political functions for the church – justifying its exclusive claims, its
authority-structure and so forth – which the new hermeneutics
conspicuously fails to do. This is what is known as 'the gap
between the church and the theologians': criticism may interpret
myth sympathetically, but it undeniably has the effect of undermining its authority-validating function. I have attempted to make
good some of the deficiency here by arguing that underlying the
traditions of the teaching of Jesus there are certain formal structures, by analysing which we can explain his work as a perennially
effective prophet of religious awakening; and that underlying the
mythicized God of everyday practical religion there is a formal *a
priori* structure of the religious life.[18] So I claimed – rather too
conservatively, perhaps – that a full acceptance of the implications
of the concept of myth need not dissolve everything away into
relativism and anthropocentrism. There are certain fixed logical

features both of Jesus' utterance and of the structure of the spiritual life. But even this is still inadequate and subversive, for it implies that the truth is *politically* quakerish rather than hierarchical and catholic.

We begin to see now how difficult is the problem of myth and consciousness. It is all very well to learn how to treat an adherent of another religion with respect, to see his practices as expressive and symbolic, to recognize his religious experience as a 'how-it-seems-to-him-in-his-tradition', to see his gods as personified religious ideals and so forth; but there are all sorts of reasons why we wish to resist the encroachment of such ways of thinking upon our own self-understanding. The concept of myth is used in an attempt to persuade us to think of our own faith in the same sort of way as we have already learned to think about other people's faiths. That is not easy to do. For example, when talking about other people's religion we ascribe to their faith the powers that they themselves attribute to their gods. We lose little by this device, for almost all the things that are said about the power of *God* to help, support and guide us can equally effectively be said about the power of *faith*. But it is not easy to carry through the implications of this realization. We resist it. We can see the force of a critical view of everybody else's faith but our own. We behave like the congregation imagined by Jonathan Swift: every member of the congregation had a tennis racket which he used to deflect the preacher's shafts onto his neighbour's head.

The last and most important defensive trick that we use to fend off the encroachment of criticism upon our own self-understanding is a version of the only-insiders-can-understand argument. The claim is that the scientific study of religion can deal only with externals. It cannot reach the inner, hidden, secret region where the believer communes in his heart with his God. That secret citadel is the last fortress of objective religious truth.

Many students of religion still treat this claim with some deference, even though it limits the scope of their subject and allows each and every sort of believer to remain entrenched in his own citadel, convinced that in the last resort he is invulnerable. Yet they should not be so deferential, for the claim is very dubious. It is only a special case of the old Cartesian doctrines that each of us has a private inner mental world of his own, and that the ultimate foundations of knowledge lie in that mental world: but modern philosophy has shown that the second of these claims is false and the first is trivial. All meanings and all knowledge are established socially, in the public world. The belief that there can be inner, ineffable private knowledge of publicly-significant truths is nonsense: you cannot claim both public truth and private validation for the same belief. It is true that the public world which we construct in our daily intercourse with each other is a network of systematically-connected points of view, rather as maps are made by triangulation; but everything that can be seen from any one point of view gets incorporated into the map through language and so made part of the public scheme of things. It is an unnecessary myth (in the popular pejorative sense of the term) to suppose that at each point of view a mind-bubble opens out off the map into another dimension, and it is confused to claim that within one particular bubble things can be seen that are important facts about the map but which are necessarily invisible from other viewpoints on the map.

In practice, few of us doubt that a discerning friend or a psychotherapist may have an understanding of us that is much superior to the understanding that we have of ourselves, and similarly one who is versed in psychological and social science may understand why a cult-member believes what he does and has the experiences that he has, better than does the cult-member himself. In at least some cases – eccentric minority cults – we do not admit that the cult-member may have esoteric and privately-validated knowledge, but on the contrary are persuaded that we can 'see through' him. And in principle it is possible that the scientific study of religion may progress far enough to produce general interpretations of religious belief, practice and experience far superior to any of the official internal theologies of religious groups. We have seen that official internal theologies in many ways function as defence-mechanisms; and why should they do that unless they are secretly afraid that they will indeed be 'seen through'?

If we admit this, then the defence-mechanisms fail. We can no longer claim to have private and inaccessible knowledge of our God which cannot be reached and explained by the demythologizing critical mind. We have no recourse left but to make that mind our own and adopt a fully critical religious self-understanding, Hyperborean faith.

That is what the concept of myth ultimately requires of us, and that is why it has been a battleground since it was first introduced into modern theology some two hundred years ago.[19] The early history is instructive.

The term myth as we now use it was invented by C. G. Heyne (1729–1812) in the heyday of the German Enlightenment, and applied by him to the old stories of the Greeks and Romans. He made a broad distinction between philosophical myths telling of the birth of the gods and the beginning of the world, historical myths about the beginnings of the people, and poetical myths which are aesthetic and expressive. He argued that myth is everywhere the oldest and most primitive form of poetry.

Within a very few years the concept of myth began to penetrate Christian theology. In his anonymous *Urgeschichte* (1779), J. G. Eichhorn (1752–1827) argued that the term was equally applicable to the ancient Hebrew stories in Genesis. With J. P. Gabler (1753–1826), Eichhorn subsequently extended the principle to the rest of the Old Testament, and then to the appearances of supernatural beings in the New Testament. Eichhorn saw myth as a primitive and unified vision of the world from which in later times philosophy, history, science, poetry and other forms of expression have branched out and become distinct from each other.

Cautious movement into the field of Christian doctrine now followed. In 1799 an anonymous work, probably by J. C. Grohmann (1769–1847), first attempted to describe how his followers had retrospectively mythicized Jesus after his death, as their yearning imaginations clothed his memory with the attributes of the supernatural Messiah and Redeemer promised of old. During the next generation others filled in more details of the Old Testament sources of the supernatural elements in the Gospels; and still there was not a public outcry, because the discussion had so far been academic and had not been aggressively obtruded upon the consciousness of the church. The storm only finally broke when D. F. Strauss (1808–1874) published in his *Life of Jesus Critically Examined* (1835) the first comprehensive and vigorously-written mythical interpretation of the Gospels. Strauss's book was certainly obtrusive, and within ten days after the first volume appeared his superiors were asking whether such views could be tolerated in one who was a tutor of candidates for the ministry. The answer was that they could not.

Strauss's mythical interpretation was in effect a naturalistic explanation, for if he was right there was no need to invoke supernatural causes to explain the contents of the Gospels. It was sufficient for him to supply an account of the original Jesus and his impact, an account of the religious ideas available to Jesus' early followers, and a theory of how the myth-making imagination works. With these materials Strauss could work out a reasonably complete historical explanation of why the Gospel story is told as it is, an explanation that does not need to invoke any special divine activity.

All this shows very clearly why the concept of myth is the thorn in the flesh of modern theology, and why it has been said that the history of myth is the history of the demythologizing of myth.[20] At first it seems odd to suggest that in demonstrating the presence of a great deal of mythical thinking in the Gospels, Strauss was in effect demythologizing them. Why should a mythical interpretation be described as *de*mythologizing? The confusion is partly due to Bultmann, for whom to recognize myth was almost the same thing as to recommend that it be discarded, whereas one might possibly do the former and not the latter. It would be clearer to say that once the modern concept of myth had been formulated and had become available to scholars as a tool of interpretation, it was bound to exert a strong secularizing influence. As Strauss himself admits, what the church calls supernatural and attributes to a special act of God, he calls mythical, and attributes it to the creative power of human religious psychology.[21] The concept of myth has a very strong 'desupernaturalizing' effect; it eats away at traditional supernatural faith by offering a naturalistic theory of how religious beliefs grow up.

A few believers were nevertheless willing to accept the use of the term myth to describe their own religious beliefs. Baden Powell, for example, described a myth as 'a doctrine expressed in a narrative form, an abstract moral or spiritual truth dramatised in action or personification', and said that 'every dogma is more or less a myth, as it is necessarily conveyed in analogical language and anthropomorphic action'.[22] But Baden Powell's religious views were almost as liberal as Matthew Arnold's; for him religion was scarcely more than righteousness in poetry. If accepting the concept of myth means going as far as *that*, then few believers have been prepared to join Baden Powell. Instead they have commonly preferred to counter-attack by objecting that the word myth is impossibly vague, for (they say) there is little agreement on the definition of myth and none at all on the relative merits of the countless theories of myth.

However, this stock objection fails. It is true that myths are very various and that no single analytical definition can compass them all, but it does not follow from this that myth is indefinable. All we have to do is to list a large number of typical features of myth, and then lay it down that a story may be called a myth if it has most of these features. There may well be no single feature that every myth possesses, but that is of no consequence provided that the broad family-resemblance among myths in general is sufficiently strong. So we may say that a myth is typically a traditional sacred story of anonymous authorship and archetypal or universal significance which is recounted in a certain community and is often linked with a ritual; that it tells of the deeds of superhuman beings such as gods, demigods, heroes, spirits or ghosts; that it is set outside historical time in primal or in eschatological time or in the supernatural world, or may deal with comings and goings between the supernatural world and the world of human history; that the superhuman beings are imagined in anthropomorphic ways, although their powers are more than human and often the story is not naturalistic but has the fractured, disorderly logic of dreams; that the whole body of a people's mythology is often prolix, extravagant and full of seeming inconsistencies; and finally that the work of myth is to explain, to reconcile, to guide action or to legitimate. We can add that myth-making is evidently a primal and universal function of the human mind as it seeks a more-or-less unified vision of the cosmic order, the social order, and the meaning of the individual's life. Both for society at large and for the individual, this story-generating function of the mind seems irreplaceable. The individual finds meaning in his life by making of his life a story set within a larger social and cosmic story.

When a story has most of the features just described, then it is a myth; and our 'family-resemblance' approach to the task of defining myth also explains why there have been so many theories of myth.[23] Most theories of myth have tried to prove that all myths must have some one essential characteristic. It is argued that every myth has to be about gods, or be linked with a ritual, or validate some social institution, or be set in primal time, and so on; and then others come along and solemnly refute the theory by quoting obvious exceptions. Our way of defining myth allows for its diversity and permits us to see each major theory of myth as making a worthwhile point even though no single theory is universally applicable.

Finally we should briefly note that there are of course many marginal cases, extended or metaphorical uses of myth that may include wartime legends, artists who died young, venerated national leaders and so on. In addition, secular stories about evolution or progress may take on the appearance and functions of myth. But these marginal cases do not affect the main point, which is that the concept of myth is as clear and useful as any other of the broad interpretative concepts used in the humanities. So what is the objection to calling Christian doctrine mythological? In the many forms in which it is presented in scripture, the creeds and worship, it satisfies nearly all of the criteria we have laid down. So why do the theological reviewers foam at the mouth and reach for their biggest guns when they read the word?

The mutual misunderstanding is sometimes comical. The anthropologist or historian of religion, who has no religious or anti-religious mission nor any personal axe to grind, uses the word myth to characterize precisely the primal and distinctively religious way of thinking. How can he be accused of secularist presuppositions when all he has done is to coin a word to pick out the specifically religious form of thought and linguistic expression? Our discussion so far suggests the answer: the believers' anger is a response to the political threat of being understood and 'seen through' from a superior vantage-point. The word 'myth' brings with it a challenge to religious change, a challenge to adopt a fully-critical religious self-understanding and a change that is terrifying in its implications.

The political threat to traditional faith was already implicit in the Enlightenment temper of mind that made it possible to frame the concept of myth in the first place. It was a temper of mind that could only have developed among people who felt they had made a decisive advance upon earlier ways of thinking and could look back with some sense of superiority upon less enlightened ages.

Nothing irks the believer more than to see a post-Enlightenment scholar pick up with his tweezers the reality that he (the believer) lives by, examine it, pickle it, label it and put it on a shelf in his intellectual museum as a quite fascinating survival of archaic ways of thinking. The scholar says and believes that his intentions are honourable and his judgments value-neutral, but the victim is not in the least mollified. He does not like to be understood from above, and put in a museum. The very act of formulating the concept of myth carries with it the suggestion that that is how *they* used to think, but not how 'we' now think; that myth is not of course factually true in the way that a statement in science or history may be; that myth belongs to the childhood of the race and the deep sub-rational levels of the mind, whereas 'we' are now adults; that myth explains animistically, whereas 'we' now explain mechanistically; that myth is poetic, expressive, anthropomorphic and projective, something 'we' may admire and look back upon with affection and nostalgia, something even that 'we' may regress to in moments of temporary weakness when we need reassurance, but nevertheless in the end something which is slipping away and cannot now regain its old authority. When people talk of myth they often do so with a suggestion that those who 'still' live enclosed within a mythical world-view are fortunate, for they have something precious which 'we' have now lost, a unified vision of the universe, society and the meaning of life. Our own culture once had such a unified vision, but since the latter Middle Ages it has slowly disintegrated as critical history has replaced myth and legend, natural science has replaced the old sacred cosmology, and so on. How sad . . . and as the believer hears all this and picks up all these faintly derogatory overtones he is confirmed in his suspicion that the concept of myth is being used as an ideological weapon. People pretend to be using the concept of myth in a neutral, descriptive sense; but in reality it comes as part of a whole mentality which is highly ideological. In that respect it is like the concept of secularization.

Hence the typical Evangelical complaint about 'presuppositions'. The traditionalist believer suspects – with some reason, it must be said – that the very invention of the concept of myth is itself a bold act of demythologizing, and unless he challenges it at once he will shortly find himself out-manoeuvred. When scholars devise a special technical jargon for explaining religion they help

to accelerate the process by which religion ceases to be something
luminously clear, with authority over all aspects of life, and
becomes instead something dark and puzzling that we need expert
help to understand.

One can sympathize with the believer's irritation with all this.
The term 'myth' does carry overtones of Enlightenment ideology,
and its coining does indeed mark the arrival of a time when
theological statements have suddenly lost intelligibility – and in
this context intelligibility *means* social authority. The newly-
dethroned Queen of the Sciences looks a pathetically vulnerable
figure. To describe her claims as 'mythical' may be an attempt to
protect her from over-rigorous historical or scientific scrutiny, but
it also draws attention to her anomalous status. In short, when
people became conscious of myth as myth, it was in some sense
left behind. By being thought, myth was encapsulated. It had lost
its old universal and unconscious dominion, and was now recognized as being just one human way of thinking among others. It is
because he senses that this is what is happening that the believer
fights back so hard.

Something similar happened in the nineteenth century with the
invention of the world 'eschatology'. The new historical consciousness had encapsulated certain old religious ways of thinking
about the Last Things, making them suddenly seem archaic and
puzzling. The word eschatology was coined in order to draw
attention to what had been lost. Thereafter theologians might
struggle to revive eschatology, and insist on how important this
particular area of religious hope and expectation is, *but the word
itself was against them.* The unlovely neologism is a grave-marker
that commemorates the death by encapsulation of a particular
area of religious language. By the time people had become
conscious of eschatology *as* eschatology they had inevitably
become conscious of it as something that had been lost.

However, all this is water under the bridge by now. The cultural
changes brought about by the Enlightenment have taken place
and appear irreversible. Large areas of religious language have
now lost social authority, and therefore intelligibility. In consequence they have been encapsulated and labelled, and their
interpretation has become the task of social anthropologists and
others. The upshot is that the old sort of dogmatic theology is
today unable to tell us much about what religion is and may

become. Critical religious hermeneutics, the critical interpretation of religion, is now far more illuminating. In the academic world, 'theology' in the old sense has by now largely been transformed – often in an unpublicized and even unconscious way – into 'religious studies' and history of religious ideas.

Suppose, then, that we adopt a fully-critical religious self-understanding: suppose that we try to reconcile myth and consciousness, enchantment and criticism? Is it possible to go all the way with the critical approach and accept that religious beliefs are indeed human products through and through, reflecting human psychology, human world-views, and human forms of social organization – is it possible to accept all this, to understand religion in a modern way, *and yet* remain a believer? Can we be justified in continuing in some sense to affirm a myth and use it instrumentally, in the full realization of its character as myth?

One answer was given recently by Maurice Wiles.[24] He says that you may continue to affirm a myth, provided that underlying it there are certain metaphysical and historical truths of which it is an appropriate symbolic expression. So it is permissible to use the creation myth insofar as we have good reasons for holding that the world is indeed 'dependent on a transcendent creative source'. We can affirm the myth of the Fall insofar as it is indeed empirically the case that men fall short of 'the highest that they see and could achieve'. We are justified in talking of the resurrection of the dead and of the last judgment insofar as there is reason for believing that 'in some sense man lives on beyond his physical death'.[25] The great christological doctrines about Jesus might similarly be kept as apt poetic expressions of the significance of the original Jesus.

Wiles' general message, then, is that we may recognize that much of Christian doctrine is mythological and affirm it as such, provided that beneath the myths there remains a foundation of ontological and empirical 'correlates' of which the myths are a poetical elaboration. He sees that it is not easy to define these correlates, nor to say just how ample they have to be in order to justify the use of the myth. The myth of the Fall of Man suggests that blameworthiness is transmissible from generation to generation, that all evil in the world is a punishment for human sin, and that one should live by an ethic of commandments. Wiles does not accept these ideas, and therefore interprets the Fall-story as simply conveying a very general message about human shortcomings. But is that enough to justify continuing affirmation of the myths of the Fall and Original Sin? Maybe not, and if so, Wiles would say that the myths should be dropped.

Another sort of disagreement about the correlates may arise in the case of the resurrection of the dead and the last judgment. For Wiles the minimal correlate here is the possibility of getting closer to God in a life beyond death, but he recognizes that some writers interpret the myths solely with reference to this present life. For them the only essential correlate is the belief that we can and should 'die' to our old selves and be reborn to a new life; that is, that we can undergo a certain moral change. How is one to decide which view of the minimum essential correlate is right, when myths are known to be so plastic, and capable of various interpretations?

Finally, in the case of Christ, what really validates the incarnation-myth for Wiles is the general possibility of fellowship and communion between the human and divine spirits. The link with Jesus is contingent, and Wiles says this because he is very well aware of the difficulty of establishing any historical statements about Jesus' personal qualities. However, he suggests that it is legitimate to tie the incarnation-myth to Jesus insofar as we have reason to think that Jesus was a man close to God whose way of living symbolized God's love for men and whose death and resurrection, enacted in sacraments, proves effective in uniting people with God.

All this implies that Wiles thinks that beneath the developed Christian mythology there is a basic non-mythological core of Christian truth, roughly as follows:

1. God is the transcendent creator of the world.
2. God loves men and desires their union with himself.
3. Men have always fallen short of what they might be, and need help to draw closer to God.
4. Jesus was a man who lived close to God.
5. Jesus' life was an acted parable of God's love for men.
6. The ritual re-enactment of Jesus' death and resurrection helps people to draw closer to God.
7. This closeness to God reaches final fulfilment after death.

And Wiles' suggestion is that we can be critically aware of the mythical character of much of the language of creed and worship and yet remain believers, provided that we have good grounds for thinking that this core-syllabus is simply true.[26]

However, these supposed rudiments of non-mythological doctrine are surely themselves just as mythological as the larger system. It is as if Wiles were saying that behind the gross myths there are thinner and more refined myths, which by being so much thinner can somehow manage to be descriptively true in a way that the gross myths cannot. Behind the gross picture of the Sky-Father setting the cosmos in order lies a refined picture of a metaphysical creator – but the notion of creation is still there, and it is still mythical. Behind the gross myth of the Son of God's descent from heaven to earth lies the more refined picture of a loving personal God who seeks to draw all men into union with himself; but the ideas of a personal God, of love and of union here drawn on are themselves mythical. The claim that Jesus' life was an acted parable of God's love amounts to saying that Jesus' life was a historically-enacted myth of the divine love. Other empirical claims, about universal human shortcomings, about Jesus' closeness to God and about sacramental efficacy, are not only difficult to verify, but need reference to myth in order to explain them. Finally, the notion of life after death is bound up with such typically mythological ideas as those of a disembodied person and of another heavenly world.

So Wiles' seven propositions are themselves thoroughly mythological. He is following an old tradition in apologetics which distinguishes between the core-syllabus and the full syllabus. The core-syllabus, as formulated within a certain group at a certain period, consists of a basic set of beliefs that are felt at the time to be reasonably secure, unproblematic and either evidently true or at least rationally defensible. The full syllabus consists of an elaborated superstructure of picturesque doctrines and practices which illustrate and confirm the core. Strategically, the apologist argues that since we, like all reasonable folk, already accept the core, it is no very great step for us to go on to accept the superstructure as well.

The content of the core-syllabus has naturally been seen very differently at different periods. In the early days the core-syllabus was Jewish faith, and later it was, for many converts, the Platonic philosophy. In more recent centuries natural theology and idealist philosophy have been popular core-syllabuses, often with a suggestion of the distinction between the kernel and the husk. Because of the influence of the notion that religion is just metaphysics in pictorial form, the kernel has been seen as a small body of universal philosophical truths, and the husk of myth and ritual has been seen as being little more than a tuppence-coloured version of them for popular consumption. It was assumed that myth and ritual are not religiously significant in their own right but have to be justified by reference to underlying metaphysical truths, an assumption that turned out to have been very damaging when it began to be realized that religion is *all* husk, myth and ritual all the way through.

So I suggest that Maurice Wiles' type of manoeuvre, which seeks to justify myth by reference to deep non-mythological truths underlying it, is counter-productive. What is more, it is an odd reversal of the natural order of things. We do not *first* find reason for believing that there is a loving God and *then* come to see that the developed myth-and-ritual complex is an acceptable pictorial representation of it. On the contrary, what draws people to religion in the first place is the developed myth-and-ritual complex; and it is only through participation in it that people come to speak of the love of God. Today, indeed, we have reason to think that what makes religion effective *as religion* is precisely the apparatus of myths, symbols and rituals that was for so long disparaged and underestimated. It now looks as if it is a mistake to suppose that religion needs to be justified from outside by being set upon a firm foundation of metaphysics and epistemology. Religion no more needs that sort of justification than does art.

This rejection of 'foundationalism' is part of a more general shift that has recently been taking place in philosophy.[27] Philosophers used to think that it was their task to provide secure intellectual foundations for all the principal branches of knowledge and areas of human activity. Philosophy had the power to set up a general metaphysical framework, to analyse how the mind does work, and to lay down how it ought to work within each area of activity. Thus philosophers were in a position to be universal policemen with authority to tell science, history, art, morality and religion what their status was, how they ought to proceed, on what foundations they rested, and how they should behave towards each other.

In recent years, however, there has been a strong reaction

against this conception of the task of philosophy. Science, art and history, for example, appear to be self-policing. They are not clamouring for philosophers to come to their aid by telling them what they are doing and how to do it. On the contrary, they evolve their own rules and criteria *ambulando*, through their continuing internal conversation among themselves. Historical study of their developing discourses shows them doing just that. So what can this extra thing called 'the mind' be, with its allegedly fixed capacities and limits to be defined by philosophers in a way that gives them the right to break into particular conversations and start laying down the law about what may and may not be said and known? On the contrary, the rules governing a particular field of discourse emerge within the practice of that discourse; and, what is still more important, discourses and the rules governing them continually evolve from within. It is for the practitioners to decide among themselves through their discourse in what way their discourse shall develop and not for philosophers to legislate to them about the path they shall be allowed to take in the future.

In this way the modern movement towards a language-centred outlook which is in broad terms naturalistic, historicist and behaviourist implies a much more modest view of the role of philosophy. With this change it becomes possible to recognize the fact that modern religious thought is abandoning theological realism and any sort of correspondence theory of religious truth. In the end you can only hold a correspondence theory of religious truth if you concede that philosophy has the ability to establish the metaphysical facts and then to assess religious language to see how far it does indeed correspond with those metaphysical facts. That, in effect, is to hand to philosophy the power to predetermine the limits of religious thought and future religious change,[28] and many philosophers now question their own authority to act in such a way. Besides, as we have seen, religious thought in modern times is progressively abandoning realism—the claim that religious statements purport to refer to and to describe supernatural facts. The internal discourse of religion is evolving, and who is to prohibit this evolution? Religious ideas are increasingly used, not as if they were speculatively-true assertions in dogmatic metaphysics, but as if their meaning is the part they play in guiding the religious life. In the end a religion is not so much a metaphysical system as a spiritual path, an ethic, a group of ideals and a way of seeing life; and as such it is something that must be chosen just for its own sake. Religion is practical, and the function of religious doctrines is to show us in condensed and symbolic form what this practical reality of religion is, and to guide us along its path. The concrete lived reality of the religious life comes first, and the doctrine is simply a mythical representation of it, framed in order to fix, preserve and communicate it so far as language is able to do so. Because doctrine is mythical, and myth is very plastic, it is capable of a great deal of reinterpretation. As times change, the conception of the religious life changes and doctrine is reinterpreted, and so continuing religious evolution is possible: though we may eventually come to a time when cultural change has gone so far and so fast that the old myths and symbols can no longer keep pace with it, and some at least of them drop out of living religious language altogether. Then we may speak of religious revolution.

The old dogmatic realism was linked with and was the ideological expression of Christianity's claim to hegemony over the whole of culture. The Enlightenment overthrew the Queen of the Sciences, and Christianity has been struggling ever since to come to terms with its loss of imperial power, social control and readily-intelligible realist doctrines. There is still a good deal of residual bitterness and longing for the return of the old régime; but at the same time there are more hopeful signs of adjustment. The image of Christ has changed a good deal: he is less of a monarch and has become a more human and more inward figure whose only power is that of example and love, the liberating power of one who opens the way to a better world. And there is a second pointer to the future in the widespread rejection of the old religious psychology. Realist faith in the past bound people together in a chain of inner bondage running down from superiors to inferiors and from generation to generation. It was locked into a masters-and-servants vision of the universe in which everyone was a divided self, both dominated and seeking to dominate in order to prolong the chain. Breaking the chain, non-realist faith promises the fulfilment of the ancient hope that the religious community might become a fellowship of freedom.

3

THE MESSAGE THAT CANNOT BE UNDERSTOOD

In the first volume of *Either/Or* Kierkegaard tells this story:

> It happened that a fire broke out backstage in a theatre. The clown came out to inform the public. They thought it was a jest and applauded. He repeated his warning, they shouted even louder. So I think the world will come to an end amid general applause from all the wits, who believe that it is a joke.[1]

What does this parable mean? There are various points in the story which our understanding might fasten upon and crystallize around – the theatre, the hidden fire, the clown, his message – but from its context in the book and from its last sentence we can be sure that Kierkegaard intended his first readers to concentrate their attention on the response of the audience to the news they hear. He is satirizing the spiritual frivolity of the Copenhagen *beau monde*. Because of who they are, the mood they are in, the place, the incongruity of the message and the appearance of the messenger they cannot respond appropriately to what they hear. Their whole life-situation is such that they cannot take in a really serious communication. There is dramatic irony in the story, because the reader observes their behaviour as if from a higher-level auditorium which reverses the relation of folly to sanity. They think it appropriate to laugh at the clown's folly, but we know that they are fools who cannot hear a sober message.

However, a modern reader cannot read the story quite as Kierkegaard's first readers were intended to read it. In Kierkegaard's language, the parable's original meaning was merely

'aesthetic', but we now perceive in it many of the deeper themes
that were to emerge in his later years. The image of the stage, the
question of whether one is a spectator of existence or an actor, the
still-hidden but fast-spreading fire, the problem of communication
and the difficulty of awakening frivolous mankind to the seriousness of existence, and the plight of the original Teacher who
cannot but appear to be a fool speaking folly – with astonishing
(and perhaps even unconscious) economy Kierkegaard evokes a
whole religious tradition and sets out the programme for his own
life's work, all in a few brief sentences. Perhaps he did tell the
story to make just one point, but his later writings have added
several extra layers to its meaning. In particular, it has become an
example of a parable that we come across from time to time, the
parable about parables, the parable about the Teacher whose
message cannot be understood however hard he tries to communicate it. Indeed, the harder he tries the more he fails.

The noblest and strangest example of this theme is perhaps the
prophet Ezekiel. He is warned from the outset that he will fail, but
he must persist with his message of judgment whether people hear
or refuse to hear, so that in the end they will know that there has
been a prophet among them.[2] God tells the prophet beforehand
that 'the house of Israel will not listen to you'; nevertheless, he is
not to flinch, for, 'Behold, I have made your face hard against
their faces, and your forehead hard against their foreheads'.[3] The
prophet is appointed to be a watchman who must simply do his
duty by sounding the alarm, regardless of whether anyone pays
heed or not. So Ezekiel does what is required of him: he delivers
oracles, preaches, tells parables – and the only result is that he
becomes a *popular preacher*! People gossip about him, and gather
round to watch him perform just as if he were an entertainer. God
remarks sardonically that, 'You are to them like one who sings
love songs with a beautiful voice and plays well on an instrument,
for they hear what you say but they will not do it'.[4] The prophet
attempts to bring about a breakthrough of understanding by
performing bizarre and outrageous parabolic actions: he scratches
a picture of the approaching siege of Jerusalem on an unbaked
clay tile, he symbolizes the coming exile by lying on his side for
hundreds of days, he cooks unclean food to eat, and he shaves his
head and burns and scatters the hair.[5] No result. He goes still
further: during one night he digs a hole through the city wall and

simply flees the city as a refugee with his bundle on his shoulder,[6] and on another occasion when his wife dies he refuses to perform the Jew's sacred duty of mourning the dead. What is one bereavement when so many are coming? [7]

In response, people say only that he is 'a maker of allegories';[8] he talks in riddles. There is no way left in which the message can be communicated. So at his furthest extremity the prophet becomes dumbstruck, and God declares that his dumbness will only be lifted when all is over and a messenger comes to report the fall of the city.[9] The last communication is silence. The prophet has something to say, something so terrible that people cannot hear it, something to which in the end he can only bear witness by his own inability even to utter it. So he is dumb, and his dumbness is itself a parabolic communication.

There is a parallel between the behaviour of Ezekiel and that of the central character in John Arden's play *Sergeant Musgrave's Dance*. Musgrave and three soldiers arrive at a Northern town in winter, ostensibly on a recruiting mission, but in fact they are deserters, obsessed by the horror of the colonial wars in which they have been fighting. The worthy townsfolk understand nothing of what they are doing by letting their young men go overseas to fight in their name. How can it be brought home to them? As Peter Brook comments,[10] Musgrave's need to communicate leads him to improvise a piece of rough popular theatre in the town market-place. For his props Musgrave uses machine-guns, flags, and a uniformed skeleton hauled aloft. But he still meets incomprehension, and in his frenzy to project his meaning he begins a rhythmic stamp which develops into a savage dance and chant. Arden has created a play within a play which is about the close affinity between religious and theatrical communication; and its subtitle actually declares *Sergeant Musgrave's Dance* to be 'An Un-historical Parable'.[11]

In the traditions about Jesus a number of fresh variations are added. It is said that the whole of his public teaching was parabolic, or at least that he never taught publicly without making some use of parables.[12] People's failure to understand Jesus is repeatedly emphasized, and many of the parables of rejection can be interpreted as being themselves parables about the failure to understand parables, and the consequent rejection of the Teacher and his message.[13] As with Ezekiel, Jesus' rejection by his own people is seen as predestined, and it can even be said that he speaks in parables *in order* to be rejected, so weighty and ineluctable a fact is the necessity of misunderstanding. The theme of the Teacher's madness appears at Capernaum when Jesus' relatives and friends attempt 'to seize him, for they said, "He is beside himself" ', while the Jerusalem scribes describe him as possessed by demons.[14] Nowadays we have learned to see Jesus as firmly rooted in the tradition of the Israelite prophets, and it has become possible to recognize that like Ezekiel he makes very extensive use of parabolic actions. Going into the wilderness, appointing twelve rulers of the twelve tribes of Israel, performing the signs of the Kingdom, holding banquets, going to Jerusalem, entering the city on an ass, cleansing the Temple, preaching on its southern steps, cursing the fig-tree – in such events, if they are historical, he may well have been deliberately performing symbolic actions which would convey to the chosen few his conviction that the Kingdom of God was at hand. Those who knew the Hebrew Bible and could make connections would grasp what he meant by what he did.

Finally, a more modern example, full of echoes of the earlier ones. In almost his last words before madness finally descended on him, Nietzsche declared: 'I refuse to be a saint; I would rather be a clown.' [15] His most famous parable, that of the Madman, has one or two trial runs in his writings,[16] but appears in its fullest form in *The Gay Science* (1882):[17]

> Have you not heard of that madman who lit a lantern in the bright morning hours, ran to the market-place, and cried incessantly, 'I seek God! I seek God!' As many of those who do not believe in God were standing around just then, he provoked much laughter. 'Why, did he get lost?', said one. . .

This is, of course, the great parable about the death of God, but it is noticeable that Nietzsche is not concerned to establish that the death of God has occurred, for the people in the market-place are *already* unbelievers. The problem is rather that they do not yet grasp the magnitude of what has happened, still less that it was they themselves who brought it about. The madman launches into a great lament:

> Where has God gone? I shall tell you. *We have killed* him – you and I. All of us are his murderers. But how have we done this?

How were we able to drink up the sea? Who gave us the sponge to wipe away the entire horizon? What did we do when we unchained this earth from its sun? Whither is it moving now? Whither are we moving now? Away from all suns? . . .

The madman cries that it is as if we have unloosed this earth from its sun and are flying rudderless through infinite nothingness. There is no up or down any more, and it is becoming steadily colder and darker: 'Shall we not have to light lanterns in the morning?' The whole structure of the cosmos is disintegrating. There can be no making atonement for such a deed; it is too great for that. Years before, the wanderer in Wilhelm Müller's poems, set to music by Franz Schubert in *Die Winterreise*, had said, 'If there is no god on earth/We are gods ourselves';[18] but Nietzsche's madman goes further than that in declaring that we shall have to become gods in order to measure up to the deed we have done. But finally the madman's outburst runs out of steam:

Here the madman fell silent and looked again at his listeners; and they too were silent and stared at him in astonishment. At last he threw his lantern on the ground, and it broke and went out. 'I come too early,' he said then; 'my time has not come yet. This tremendous event is still on its way, still wandering – it has not yet reached the ears of man. Lightning and thunder require time, the light of the stars requires time, deeds require time even after they are done, before they can be seen and heard. This deed is still more distant from them than the most distant stars – *and yet they have done it themselves.*'[19]

I have stressed that the parable is not about the death of God but about how difficult it is for people who are *already* unbelievers to grasp the full implications of their own unbelief. In itself the theme of the death of God was far from new. It is to be found in Jean Paul's novel *Siebenkäs* of 1796, and more or less contemporaneously in the eccentric English poet William Blake; Hegel used the phrase in an essay on 'Faith and Knowledge' in 1802 and discussed the idea in his *Lectures on the Philosophy of Religion*;[20] and Heinrich Heine has a celebrated passage about it in his articles on *Religion and Philosophy in Germany*,[21] which first appeared in Paris in 1833. In writers of the Romantic generation there is often a sense of release and exaltation as the divine, no longer exclusively concentrated in a single transcendent focus, becomes naturalized, enters man himself and is diffused through all experience. Turning from the Jews to the Greeks, we can become godlike ourselves and learn to see divinity in all things. There was in most minds a general presumption that though the old God might die, the world, the moral order and man would stand firm without him. But for Nietzsche, this 'semi-nihilism' was illusory and could only be a transitional phase. When the consequences of their deed finally caught up with its perpetrators they would have to go through to the far side of nihilism proper, and Nietzsche set out to chart the way. He is a man describing a fearful journey ahead to a generation of people who are still comfortable in their old homes and have as yet no idea that they will shortly be compelled to leave. To them, he sounds crazy; hence the parable of the madman.

Although some similarities are now beginning to appear, many people will still think that Nietzsche's message about the death of God is the direct opposite of the traditional biblical and Christian message. The prophets and Jesus had proclaimed the coming of God in judgment, with a consequent collapse of the civil and religious order that people relied on to shape their lives; and they demanded that their hearers should 'turn', repent and choose a new life. Kierkegaard launched a ferocious attack on objectified Christianity, the Christian social order or 'Christendom', as spiritually bankrupt, in order to summon people to a truly subjective Christian existence.[22] In apparent contrast, Nietzsche was saying that with the death of God in the modern period we have finally lost the traditional belief in the cosmos as a house with rules, an objective framework of physical and moral order, meanings and values. We have arrived at nihilism; and he prophesied two centuries of turmoil while people struggle to come to terms with what has happened.[23] We are just completing the first of those two centuries, and are wondering if our race will survive to complete the second.

Nietzsche, who ended by calling himself the Antichrist, was aware of an ironical affinity between himself and Jesus the Christ. Before Jesus all human life was lived under the dominion of sin, and Nietzsche similarly claims that all human life was steeped in falsehood before the will to truth at last became fully conscious of itself in his own time and his own thinking. Each of the four parabolic teachers we have mentioned – Ezekiel, Jesus, Kierkegaard and Nietzsche – was a 'madman', an 'exception', with a sense of extraordinary crisis. In each case the Teacher seeks to awaken his audience to the total insecurity of their lives. That which they think gives shape and meaning to their lives is in fact illusory or on the brink of disintegration, and they do not see the chasm before their feet. They are stuck in false consciousness, and the Teacher administers shock treatment in order to rouse them. The first two were men of the spoken word; the latter two introduced many of the techniques of the spoken language into literature in order to tease, beguile or bludgeon the reader into spiritual awakening, and wrote books that are intentionally gruelling to read.

Modern religion is too often preoccupied with dispensing consolation and prolonging the life of reassuring illusions. The good pastor is one who speaks words of comfort, and pastoral efficacy has become so much the criterion of truth that it is hard now even to make the point that the great religious teachers of the past began with the bad news. Comfort turns men into sheep, and only bad news can turn sheep into men: comedy may beguile, but only tragedy can reconcile and heal. It is typical of major religious innovators that they set out to undermine our false confidence and communicate to us a sense of impending annihilation and utter meaninglessness. The principle also applies outside the tradition within which we are speaking, for Hinduism saw the world as a wheel of becoming from which one should seek release, the Buddha sees all human life as conditioned by futile craving and suffering, and Muhammad the prophet warns of impending divine judgment. Naturally, people everywhere hate to come to the realization of the meaninglessness of their lives, for they rightly fear it more than anything else in the world and they put up a stiff resistance. It is not just that they do not happen to have ears to hear, but that they are quite determined not to have ears to hear. Nevertheless the Teacher persists, for he knows that it is only by experiencing complete breakdown and dereliction that people can be forced to repent, to change and to choose a new mode of existence on the far side of death and nothingness. The kind of inner change that religion requires of us is so drastic that we will only risk it when it is our last hope because all else is lost. Hence the symbolism of Christ's death and rebirth, and the emphasis on

Christ's exemplary cry of dereliction, his death, burial and descent into Hell. You must touch bottom. Nietzsche believed that St Paul had permanently corrupted the meaning of Jesus' death, and so he rejected the Christian way to rebirth; but he still had to have the symbolism of death and resurrection, and he projected it instead upon the figure of Dionysus.

The two great nineteenth-century prophets, Kierkegaard and Nietzsche, gave rather different diagnoses of the crisis in modern culture. Kierkegaard lived early in the century, under the shadow of Hegel's great systematic philosophy. The industrial revolution, modern liberal democracy, and the explosive growth of scientific knowledge were getting under way. Objectified and impersonal techniques and forms of understanding were becoming dominant in the culture, and the individual was becoming lost in the 'world-historical'. People were settling for mediocrity, content to feel that they were part of the vast progressive forward movement of the race. Quality was being replaced by quantity, and individual passion, inwardness and subjectivity were departing from the world. The churches shared in the general debasement, asking of their members no more than a placid bourgeois conformity and orthodoxy, and giving them in return nothing more than a foolish feeling of self-satisfaction.

In such a world real faith could not exist. Kierkegaard set out to rediscover Christian spirituality by spelling out the full demand of the gospel upon the single individual in his relation to existence. He declared war upon science, democracy, the world-historical, progress, objectivity – upon everything that might distract the individual from his solitary task of becoming an individual. He is a good deal bolder and more radical in his theology than his commentators realize, for he is saying that today the reality of God *is identical with* the awesome challenge and promise of the task of becoming an individual: 'God *is* that all things are possible';[24] 'The consciousness of being an individual, which is fundamental in man, *is* his consciousness of eternity.' [25] To reject objectivity and declare that in subjectivity alone is truth is in effect to say that to believe in the right thing is nothing but to believe in the right way, for there is no truth in Christianity that can be grasped independently of the form of existence that it requires of us. At the end of the *Postscript* he makes the point by saying that 'a man merely by describing the "how" of his inwardness can show indirectly that he is a Christian without mentioning God's name',[26] and in a journal entry he comments: 'There is a "how" which has this quality, that if *it* is truly given, then the "what" is also given'.[27] It seems from this that Kierkegaard, at least when speaking through this pseudonym, is approaching a fully non-cognitive and voluntarist philosophy of religion which identifies the meaning of a theological statement with the spirituality that it prescribes. Objectified Christianity is a contradiction in terms, for Christianity *is* that one is called to a certain mode of existence. Faith is not an affirmation that something is descriptively the case, but an infinite passion of inwardness.[28]

Kierkegaard's language is often difficult and even stilted, but then language had by his time already become so infiltrated by the objective scientific way of speaking that withholds any deep self-involvement in one's own utterance, that the Christian categories could no longer easily be expressed in it. His books are not intended to pipe a smooth flow of painless information into the reader, but to 'wound from behind'. They are meant to hurt. So he had to struggle endlessly with questions of literary technique and the theory of religious communication. There is a risk that we may become fascinated with his technique, and forget the fact that more than any other writer he sees that he is charged with the task of communicating a message that logically cannot be 'understood', because it can only be acted upon. He even rejected the desire to be understood, and set out at the end to provoke misunderstanding, rejection and hostility on the ground that by their active rejection of him people would at least indicate that they had an inkling of what his writings required of them. In a way, flat rejection of him is a less profound misinterpretation of Kierkegaard than is academic exegesis of him.

Nietzsche lived after Darwin and was twelve years older than Freud. Though he had an odd view of Darwin, he early came to accept the bleak post-Darwinian view of man's place in the universe and the limits of his intellectual powers:

> In some remote corner of the universe, poured out and glittering in innumerable solar systems, there once was a star on which clever animals invented knowledge. That was the haughtiest and yet most mendacious minute of world history – yet only a

minute. After nature had drawn a few breaths the star grew cold, and the clever animals had to die.[29]

At the end of the century the problems had changed, and the vast body of objectified scientific man-made knowledge was beginning to destroy itself. At a popular level, this could be seen happening as man began to put himself under his own microscope and to discover his own insignificance in the history of the universe, his recent and lowly origins, and the primacy of the irrational in his own nature. The latest discovery of proud human reason is our own insignificance and irrationality. The weakest of animals, the only thing that man has in him to help him make his life possible and bearable is the fantasizing power which manifests itself in our most spontaneous activities – dreaming and day-dreaming, children's play and artistic creation. If we really knew some ultimately-important truth, would we not tell it *first of all* to our children? But how do we in fact form their minds? – By telling them *fairytales*! The tallest tale is the deepest truth, for the mind lives by story-making and all our knowledge-systems and social institutions rest in the end on socially-agreed protective fictions. More philosophically, the criticism of knowledge and of our knowing powers leads in the end to scepticism about human reason; and here Nietzsche was (independently, as it seems) arriving at much the same conclusion as Hume had reached a century-and-a-half earlier. Our knowledge may appear pretty good so long as we only look outwards but, says Hume, when we examine our knowing powers, and then at a second stage ask about the adequacy of that examination, we embark upon a regress of ever-increasing doubt:

> When I reflect on the natural fallibility of my judgment, I have less confidence in my opinions, than when I only consider the objects concerning which I reason; and when I proceed still further, to turn the scrutiny against every successive estimation I make of my faculties, all the rules of logic require a continual diminution, and at last a total extinction of belief and evidence.[30]

Reason is thus reduced to irrationality: it is 'nothing but a wonderful and unintelligible instinct in our souls';[31] it 'furnishes invincible arguments against itself',[32] and at the end of the day we have 'no choice left but betwixt a false reason and none at all'.[33]

In thus emphasizing the limits of reason and the need at last to fall back upon 'nature' and the passions, Hume is close to Nietzsche, despite the superficial contrast between the cool Scottish sceptic and the overheated German late-Romantic.

There is also a similarity between them in their moral philosophies. Both are 'emotivists'; that is, they deny that there are any objective moral qualities or relations out there in the world prior to our arrival on the scene, and instead they see our moral evaluations as expressing our own emotional response to things and events. The raw material out of which morality is made is our own likes and dislikes, pleasures and pains. How then does morality come to seem so objective and authoritative? There are two main reasons. The first is that moral thinking is mythopoeic: we project our feelings about things outwards and so come to regard them as objective qualities of those things. We spread our feelings over things, and by so doing order the world in terms of the desirable and the undesirable. To evaluate is to create;[34] our valuations not only show what we are, but also are our primary way of constructing and responding to our environment. It is in this way that we make our world habitable as a scene for action. The second reason why morality seems objective is that it is necessary for social life that there be sympathy. We must learn *shared* patterns of response if there is to be speedy and coordinated common action. So morality comes to take the form of a public moral order, binding all to feel and judge as much alike as is practicably possible. Here the pressure of society and language to conformity is at odds with the philosopher's will to truth. Hume's response to this realization is cool, but then he perhaps never expected that the majority of mankind could ever come to share it. Nietzsche's response is a burning sense of crisis. The will to truth has now demythologized everything. Modern culture has been becoming more and more anthropocentric ever since the time of Descartes, and now people in general are beginning to break through to a conscious realization that there is no reality but human creative activity and the fictions it generates. For him the death of God means that we now cannot but 'see through' every kind of idealism and every vision of the moral order and the world-order. We are led to realize that all human life hitherto has been lived under unconscious domination by illusions. Nihilism has come, a condition of extraordinary novelty and freedom

which will require the greatest courage of us. At this point
Nietzsche is very like an eschatological prophet: he foretells the
annihilation of the old world and a period of apocalyptic up-
heavals before a new humanity can come to birth. First the age of
the camel, the beast burdened with the weight of 'Thou shalt';
then the age of the lion, battling against the 'Thou shalt' for the
freedom to create; and finally the coming of the new-born child.[35]
Nietzsche insists that his doctrine is not just scepticism, and not
just the pessimistic nihilism of emptiness that he found in Schopenhauer and the Buddha. Nor is it the destructive nihilism of the
young men of St Petersburg who are described in Turgenev's novel
Fathers and Sons. Nietzsche claims to announce a nihilism more
thoroughgoing than any of those, which will entirely free us from
any regrets over what we have lost, any feeling that things ought
to be other than they are, any hankering after an objectively-given
world order and moral order. His message 'cannot be understood',
because it envisages the end of our existing language, meanings
and categories of understanding, and Nietzsche himself is in the
difficulty that the only language available to him has all the old
fictions built into it. Like the man emerging blinking from Plato's
cave, he needs a new language to describe the new reality – and he
does not have it. He has to do his best with the old language, used
with considerable violence. Unhappily, so far as we can make out
what he is saying, the new ethic of the Superman which will
emerge after the revaluation of all values is neither as new nor as
attractive as it should be, and its less-appealing features have cast
a cloud over the other and more important aspects of his
philosophy.

But setting aside this last point, the resemblance to Jesus is
strong. For Jesus vigorously proclaimed the end of the world and
the coming of a new era in which religion would cease to be a
burdensome external demand and would become instead an inner
spirit of liberty. Mankind would come of age and a new humanity
would be born.

Unfortunately Nietzsche lived before the modern rediscovery
of the Jewishness of Jesus, his continuity with the prophets and
his eschatological message. Although he can briefly recognize in
Jesus one who is no respecter of persons and cares nothing for
what is fixed or established but is a 'free spirit',[36] his dominant
image of Jesus is 'feminine' in the most objectionable nineteenth-

century sense. For Nietzsche reality, so far as one may speak of 'reality' at all, is a theatre of conflict between wills-to-power. But Jesus was an absolute pacifist – and therefore in Nietzsche's view one who rejects reality, who will not stand up for himself but retreats from conflict and cannot bear even to be touched. Withdrawn into an inner manic condition of ecstatic bliss, the Kingdom of Heaven, he overcomes all painful distinctions, so that for him there is no distance between God and man, no sense of sin, no law, no punishment, no longing for forgiveness. The gospel is that one should live in a state of paradisal innocence and bliss, and it brought to an end the old Jewish theology of law, sin and expiation. Thus the true and original forgiveness of sins was an inner condition that had left the very concepts of law and sin far behind. But the crucifixion brought this original gospel to an end, for it was St Paul who by interpreting Jesus' death as a *sacrifice* reintroduced the categories of the old vengeful Jewish theology and transformed Christianity into a religion of self-punishment and resentment which was the opposite of Jesus' original gospel. The later back-projection of the early Christian religion of vengefulness into the gospel records accounts for the harsh, denunciatory and apocalyptic elements in the tradition of Jesus' words as we now have it.

Like all who doubt whether any truly historical portrait of Jesus can be recovered and confine themselves to forming a psychological impression,[37] Nietzsche saw Jesus in terms of the religious psychology of his own time – in his case, the late nineteenth century. It is a psychology full of stereotypes of masculine aggression, feminine submissiveness, patriarchal sternness, childhood innocence and Jewish deviousness, in which the praise of pure love and childlike faith coexists with inner alienation and the desire to dominate others, and for which Jesus is a sexually-ambiguous figure, a victim who attracts cruelty. In preaching we are invited to see ourselves equally ambiguously, both as crucifying him and as suffering with him. Since this is a religious psychology which still in some degree afflicts us,[38] Nietzsche's polemics against it may still have an uncomfortable ring of truth. But it is a truth about us rather than about Jesus and Paul, and if Nietzsche had lived in other and better days he might have seen the possibility of a revolutionary interpretation of Christianity as the culmination of his teaching.

In the cases we have been considering there have been slight differences in the reasons why the Teacher's message cannot be understood. Sometimes the obstacle is of a moral kind, and sometimes its character is logical. For Ezekiel, people did not want to hear about God's judgment on their folly and irrationality and could not appreciate the magnitude of the national disaster that was surely impending. For Jesus, the irony was that the Jewish religion was so geared up to waiting and expectation that in the end it could not endure the fulfilment of its own hopes. Mediated religion starts as a second-best, something transitory, but in time it becomes all that people know and all they want to know, and a class of religious professionals grows up with a strong vested interest in its continuance, come what may. What a bitter irony, that one should become so fixed in a posture of expectant hope that one cannot accept the arrival of the very thing that one was hoping for but must instead greet it with incomprehension, hatred and rejection! For Kierkegaard the problem is to avoid getting himself made into the subject of an academic industry. He knows very well that professorial commentators will pick over his bones, but that kind of understanding of him is a *mis*understanding. He does not write to be 'understood' but to change his reader, to tempt him out into Christian existence. Finally, for Nietzsche the coming of that fearsome unthing, nihilism, presents us with nothing that we can understand. It is an experience that we must go through in order to come to a new kind of life on the far side of it. All Nietzsche has for expressing his message is the common language, which is systematically misleading; so he has to do violence to it in a most unphilosophical way – and one which has long clouded his reputation – to make his point as best he can.

It is clear that for Kierkegaard and Nietzsche the obstacles to understanding are rather more *logical* in kind than they were for the old prophets. Kierkegaard believes that the dominance of objectifying scientific ways of thinking and speaking has distracted people from the urgent existential questions of life to such an extent that they can scarcely even become aware of them any more. Nietzsche thinks that the common language has an illusory world-view built into it, which surrounds us with protective fictions and prevents us from realizing the sheer nakedness of our human predicament.

The radical theologian is in a somewhat similar position. The

Christian public, and perhaps still more the half-Christian public, think they know what Christianity is and suppose the language of traditional supernatural faith to be intelligible because it is familiar, because it is consoling and because it is at least a treasured souvenir of the past. The last thing they want to hear is that this language is now outworn, that clearly we do not in fact understand it because it is only too apparent that we are not able to put it to effective and liberating use any more, that all too often we use it as a protective illusion, that it would be more truthful to discard almost all of it and admit that a new age has arrived in which we see nothing clearly and must start all over again, and finally that if we could only give up Christian illusions and instead actually rediscover Christian existence, then we might get ourselves into the right position to start forging a new kind of Christian language that would be more truthful and a more adequate vehicle for expressing where we are now and what we are now. Who wants to hear all that – and who has the literary gifts to communicate such a message? Nobody. And if someone could articulate such a message, would not all the familiar political mechanisms for protecting the status quo immediately come into operation to neutralize it? Of course they would. So I am thankful that I can manage nothing better than the plainest, stupidest prose sketch.

Since the middle of the nineteenth century there has occurred an enormous enlargement of our understanding of ourselves and the universe in which we are set. Today we have knowledge of events over distances ranging from 10^{-16}cm. to 10^{+28}cm. and over time-intervals ranging from 10^{-24}sec. to 10^{+17}sec.,[39] and new theoretical developments under active discussion among physicists seem likely greatly to extend at least the lower limits. All events in this immense ocean of phenomena seem to involve a very small number of ultimate particles and to be governed by an even smaller number of forces. Indeed one form of Grand Unified Theory suggests that at a sufficiently high energy-level, nowhere to be found in the present universe but existing at about 10^{-40}sec. after the Big Bang, one may speak in terms of a single particle and a single force.[40] Yet during the course of the universe's long history extremely complex objects have evolved out of these simple constituents. During the last forty years or so astronomy, physics, chemistry and biology have been merging together, and the story of cosmic evolution from the limit of the knowable, the Big Bang, to the emergence of human history is being constructed in a detail that would have seemed incredible only a lifetime ago. Whether we consider the story of life on earth, or the history of our species, or simply the development of science, the pattern is the same: slow beginnings are followed by steadily-accelerating change, until in the present century modern man has come into a new kind of understanding of himself and his place in the universe which has made obsolete all previous world-views.[41]

At the same time and in parallel with the emergence of this modern cosmology, there has also developed the modern secular and naturalistic understanding of human history and social life. In the old days the great cultural formations such as language, the social order, religion and knowledge-systems used to be seen as having come down from heaven and as being validated from above by supernatural authority, but now they are instead seen as having been generated from below by human social interaction. The meanings of all words and sentences are not invisible essences laid up in a Platonic heaven, but are given by the part they play in social life and the rules governing their use, rules which have been evolved through our daily intercourse with each other over the generations.

During the present century social change in general and scientific knowledge in particular have grown so fast as to raise a question about the objectivity of our knowledge. Between Newton and Einstein cosmology had remained on the whole remarkably stable for two centuries, and this stability suggested to many that scientific theory might be objectively and descriptively true of the world. But in this century all theory has everywhere been subject to continual and animated debate. With the explosively rapid growth of our knowledge has come also an awareness of its provisional, shifting and merely man-made character. The most highly-developed and mathematical sciences, cosmology, astronomy and physics, are the most aware of the limits of our knowledge. The brighter the circle of light, the deeper the encompassing darkness. Beyond the range of present theory, and perhaps beyond the scope of any theory, seem to lie questions that we do not know even how to frame properly, much less how to answer. But broadly speaking, the view of knowledge held among the leading thinkers is naturalistic: the only sound way we have of explaining any phenomenon in nature is to show that in its setting and its relations with other events in nature it exemplifies a regular pattern, preferably one that can be described in the language of mathematics. In the most complex matters, and especially in human affairs, we have to be content with something a good deal less exact than that, but we still explain in terms of regular patterns and models. And this view of knowledge, besides being natural-istic, is also man-centred, with a strong emphasis on social agreement and historical change.

So we have come by now to a completely secular view of the world and our place in it. Our new world-view has two poles. If we start from the objective pole, we disregard any worries about the precise nature of our knowledge-systems and our own faculties and simply attend objectively to what they disclose to us, and we see the universe as continuous natural process out of which we have emerged into consciousness and knowledge of our situation in a way that seems to be fully explicable in natural terms. If we start from the subjective pole we draw back and consider our-selves, and we find that we are social beings for whom all meanings, all truth, all knowledge-systems are generated by social agreement in the course of our ceaseless struggle to secure common and effective understanding and control of the world about us. Most physical scientists live habitually at the objective pole, and most social scientists live at the subjective pole. If we take account of both poles we note that although our knowledge now grows so fast, the very facts of its rapid change and its relativity to our needs and interests are a warning that the ultimate nature of things remains hidden from us.

It will certainly take a long time for people to digest all this, and it is scarcely surprising that reactions to it are very varied. Some are optimistic, claiming that man is now reborn as he emerges at last from the dreams of mythology to a clearer self-awareness and a truer recognition of his place in the world. Others are disinter-estedly absorbed in the work of advancing knowledge. Others again are pessimistic, seeing mankind as a drifting speck in a vast unmeaning universe that begot him by a series of chances and will in the end indifferently annihilate him. Among these pessimists are those religious believers who perceive the new scientific world-view as a mortal enemy. In the leading scientific country, the USA, a large section of the population is still fighting the

century-old battle against Darwinism. We should not write them
off as fundamentalist eccentrics: on the contrary, their desperation
bears witness to their entirely just sense of the greatness of the
issues involved. Perhaps the only reason why Britain is not racked
by similar controversies is that the mass of the population have
not yet fully appreciated what has happened.

That there is indeed something very odd about the cultural
situation in Britain is indicated by the fact that so many intellectuals seem to hold that the world-view of the English Common
Prayer Book of 1661/2 is still appropriate today, and have fought
so hard for the retention of that book. The Prayer Book was
published just as the Royal Society was founded, at a time when
the scientific revolution was secure; but having been over a century
in the making it takes no account of these recent developments,
and instead (like Milton's *Paradise Lost*, which appeared in the
same decade) it remains one of the last great monuments of the
old Western Christian world-view.

The Prayer Brook's language and symbolism are rooted in the
ancient picture of the universe as a hierarchically-ordered earth-
centred cosmos with three main zones. In the heavens above, God
reigns over all with his angels and the blessed dead. Below in the
infernal regions Satan rules. In the intermediate zone of earth all
significant natural events are seen as directly caused by God.
Disease and famine are regarded as divine visitations, God directly
controls the weather and fertility, kings rule on earth by divine
permission and the outcome of their wars is in his hands. As the
result of a primal sin committed by our first parents soon after the
creation of the visible world some five-and-a-half thousand years
ago, all human beings are conceived and born in sin and are
subject to continual temptation by Satan and his servants. Though
Satan's powers are merely psychological, they are sufficient to
threaten us with eternal damnation, for human nature is radically
corrupt and man has no power of himself to help himself. To limit
the destructive potential of evil, absolute monarchy is the appropriate form of government at the national as well as at the cosmic
level, and in domestic life men must correspondingly rule women
and parents rule children. Indeed, the divinely-ordained authority
of superiors over inferiors is the key organizing principle of the
whole universe, and it extends into human psychology, because
the quiet and peaceable life which represents the Prayer Book

ideal is only to be achieved by a continual crucifying of one's lower carnal nature. In an unstable, violent and evil world the maintenance of tight discipline in the self and society is seen as essential for survival.

Deeply pessimistic though the Prayer Book is, man is by no means without hope. In the earliest times God chose his ancient people the Jews to be a light to the nations, and revealed his will to them through many spokesmen. Of this people and in fulfilment of old prophecies was born in due time the Messiah of Israel, the promised Redeemer, God's Son incarnate. He freely bore the punishment for our sins in his death and raises believers to new life through his resurrection. Through faithful and obedient membership of the church that he founded men may hope to gain eternal blessedness. This life is brief and this world is evil. Judgment is near and the whole of world-history will soon be terminated by God. Christ will return to complete his conquest of evil, Satan will be sealed for ever in Hell with the souls of the damned, and the faithful will enter their everlasting rest. Meanwhile it behoves believers to live quietly within the existing social and ecclesiastical order, sustained by a confident and tranquil hope of their eternal reward.

Such is the faith of the Prayer Book. Although in 1662 it was already a little archaic, and although it so strongly reflects the political interests of the people who imposed it, it was nonetheless still broadly true to the realities of life and the way most people saw the world at the time when it was first issued. But if we compare it with the modern world-picture that I sketched at the beginning we can gain some idea of the sheer magnitude of the intellectual revolution that we have gone through, and the challenge that confronts modern theologians.

How does it come about that so many people today wish to maintain the Prayer Book's outlook intact? I do not know how far they themselves sincerely believe in the supernaturalist world-view, the principle of absolute monarchy, the direct divine causation of human sickness, the subjection of women, and the six-thousand-year time-scale. On points of that kind they must answer for themselves; but I suspect that many of them are people for whom religious faith is almost the same thing as a sense of the past, and who fear that if we wholly lose touch with that ancient world-view we will lose our cultural and religious identity. The

modern scientific outlook is felt to be deeply threatening, and the
Prayer Book represents our own childhood, a way back to the lost
sacred. If we surrender it we will become like the peoples of certain
newly-settled and revolutionary countries, peoples of the modern
age who have no past.

So strongly do they feel this that they bitterly attacked even the
Alternative Service Book of 1980 as being too modernizing. Yet
if we examine that new book we find that the ancient world-view
has not in fact been discarded, but on the contrary has been
preserved almost unchanged. There have indeed been some modest reductions in God's direct control of natural phenomena, in
the role of Satan, in the pessimism about human nature, in the
subjection of women and in the principle of absolute sovereignty.
God appears less in the likeness of an omnipotent monarch and
more in the likeness of a patient and merciful fatherly love. One
effect of these changes is that the dramatic representation of the
conflict of good with evil in human life is noticeably less grand
and vivid than it used to be; but since scripture dominates in the
new book at least as much as it did in the old, the main framework
of supernatural belief is unaltered. We still read the biblical
creation stories without any hesitation, still see the key to all life
in a series of great moments of miracle and revelation in ancient
Jewish history, still look up to another world as our true home
and ask of this world little more than that it be peaceful, and still
look for the return of Christ and a speedy supernatural end to
history. It is hard to find in the new book any evidence of the
typical concerns of the modern world, and I have searched in vain
for any acknowledgment of the development of the natural and
social sciences and the unprecedented technical control over
nature that science has brought, of the coming of modern democracy and the world-wide struggle for human rights, of the existence
of other faiths and ideologies competing for men's allegiance, or
even of biblical criticism. In doctrine and world-view, it is difficult
to imagine a more timorous revision of the liturgy, and yet even
this book aroused a storm of protest—especially from *intellectuals*!

How could such a thing be? It may be that those who fought for
the retention of the old book are themselves only too well aware
that the sacred has been lost in the modern period, and have
concluded that the only sort of religion possible today is one that
is mediated by past forms. But such a religion of nostalgia, reached

by a willed suspension of disbelief and an imaginative return to a lost age, is accessible only to those with some literary education, and it is hard to see how it can be spiritually and morally effective in anyone. And over us all there still hangs the one great fact of the chasm between the old faith and the new world. Conservative theology may represent one possible response to it, but there are two other responses that will also deserve mention.

Conservative theology, as we have seen, strives to maintain the traditional faith intact, if necessary by resorting to ever more authoritarian arguments and methods. The beliefs of the church, it is said, are like the rules of a club, and the rules must be kept. If you do not like the rules, you can always leave the club. But this line of argument, with its stress on authority and obedience, subverts the conservatives' own case, for it means that they themselves come to treat their own doctrines less and less as genuinely descriptive assertions and more and more as just – rules. If they protest that this is not so because they continue to hold as a matter of obedience that the doctrines really are descriptive, they still face the difficulty that faith becomes more and more a closed circle of ideas, intelligible only to insiders, that can no longer be connected convincingly with the ways in which meanings and truths are established in the surrounding culture. Christian doctrine becomes no more than the private code of a ghetto.

Liberal theology owes much to Hegel and Schleiermacher, and flourished in the generation before the First World War. It then went out of fashion for forty years, but has recently shown fresh signs of life. It is traditional at least in the sense that it still seeks an overall cosmological synthesis, restating the faith in a form in which it can be amalgamated with the scientific world-picture. It largely gives up the old supernaturalism and instead sees the whole mighty cosmic and historical process as a progressive self-expression of God. The old doctrines of creation, providence and redemption are all subsumed into the vision of a universe evolving onwards and upwards into ever-greater complexity and perfection. Collaborating with this great movement and increasingly inspired by Jesus' ethic of love, human history moves towards a future consummation, the New Jerusalem, the Kingdom of God on earth.

Theologies of this general type are to be found today among the followers of Teilhard de Chardin, of process theology, and of the various forms of post-Hegelian theism advocated in Germany, the USA and Britain. Such theologies exude cosmic optimism and have largely given up the old faith's powerful mythicization of the conflict between good and evil in the human soul. Instead they claim to perceive the working out of a benevolent purpose in the overall movement of cosmic and human history. But when Julian Huxley greeted Teilhard as an ally it became apparent how little difference there is between secular and religious forms of cosmic optimism; and when P. B. Medawar sharply attacked Teilhard in a famous review[42] it was clear that the modern scientific world-picture strongly resists being converted into a new form of religious mythology. Liberal optimism blows up to a cosmic scale the Whig view of history as a mighty movement culminating in ourselves, but where is the hard evidence for the purposive guidance of cosmic evolution and a man-centred view of that purpose? Scientists are suspicious, because all their past achievements have been based on rejecting vitalism and following the path of number and mechanism. They will not hastily readmit vitalism now. And that means that the old kind of unified vision is no longer possible.

We are left with the rank outsider, radical theology, which asks, How is it possible to be a Christian *at all* today, in the world we have now come to? Radicals accept that there has taken place a great and irreversible change in the human situation, and they believe that the old faith will have to undergo not just minor revisions, but a major transformation. The inner spirit of religion must be preserved, but it can only be preserved at the price of a very considerable change in our ways of thinking. And the main reason why this change is forced upon us is the loss of the supernatural world. As the course of this world became gradually more completely explicable in purely natural terms there was less and less need to appeal to supernatural agency. One can describe how and why other people in the past believed in supernatural causes of events, but it has become increasingly difficult to think in such ways oneself, today. As our ideas of knowledge and meaning became more man-centred, more historical and eventually more sociological, it became harder to see how our knowledge could ever extend beyond the world of experience or how we could speak meaningfully of an invisible supernatural world. Certainly we are surrounded by great mysteries, and certainly there may be an ultimate World-Ground unknown to us; but it *is* unknown, and we clearly perceive how far ideas about it held in the past were shaped by human needs and social conditions.

The old supernatural world faded away. How was religious thought to respond? There were two main options. Hegel and the liberals kept the cosmic side of religious belief. They have tended to identify the activity of God with the totality of the way things actually go. Redirected towards this world, religious thought and feeling tended to merge the ideal and the actual, the perfect world and the real world, and the divine love with the depths of human love. Pantheism was kept at bay by the claim that God was more than just the totality of the way the world is – but he was *only a little bit* more. Liberal theology kept sliding into an optimistic cosmic religiosity which had lost the old stringency of the religious demand and the dramatic conflict between holy God and sinful man, and was therefore rightly judged to be weak and woolly as religion.

The alternative way, beginning with Kierkegaard, was to give up the cosmic and metaphysical side of religion and to internalize faith. Kierkegaard kept the old Protestant language and its dramatic mythology, and cashed it in terms of the human being's struggle to become a fully-individuated spiritual subject. He may have relinquished the objective side of religious belief, but so far as the inner life of the individual and the moral demand of love were concerned he retained the Christian categories intact.

Radical theology follows Kierkegaard in holding that religious meaning can no longer be convincingly located *either* in a supernatural world above *or* in the natural process of this world. Instead, it must now be sought within the individual human subject. However, Kierkegaard maintained the traditional Western Christian religious psychology unaltered, for he lived before the age of Darwin, Nietzsche and Freud. Today we have to pass through the fire of their criticism, and that will require us to go a long, long way beyond Kierkegaard's position.

It is as if the ideas of certain old mystics had come true, and the Age of the Spirit has arrived. In the Age of the Father, the old covenant, God was a fearsome cosmic sovereign and judge of all, whose demand upon men was experienced as an externally-imposed and eternally-binding Law. In the Age of the Son, the New Covenant, God was incarnate in the world, and the religious

demand required membership in and allegiance to a supernatural
Body of Christ, a divine society established in history. But in the
Age of the Spirit God is poured out within each human heart.
Man can become fully liberated and self-possessed, for God is
precisely the principle in us that requires of us the highest
fulfilment of our potential for consciousness, freedom, and creative, loving self-expression.

In the Age of the Father the religious demand makes man a
servant, whose whole reason for existence is that he should do the
will of Another. In the Age of the Son the religious demand is
partly internalized, with the effect of producing a divided self
locked in the continual (and admittedly, often very creative) inner
conflict between flesh and spirit that St Paul first described. In the
Age of the Spirit man at last achieves fully unified and liberated
selfhood, for the religious demand upon us no longer divides the
self but precisely coincides with the self's struggle for spiritual
individuation.

Radicals therefore see the movement of the Spirit in today's
world in the universal struggle for education, for emancipation
and for human rights. They see religion less in terms of an external
doctrinal framework and more in terms of spirituality. But the
function of a modern spirituality is not to make us into good
servants, not to conform human life to a mythical picture of the
cosmic order, and not to dramatize and intensify inner conflict.
Rather, a modern spirituality must teach us to accept and make
the most of our new sense of ourselves and our place in nature.
The pessimists whom we mentioned earlier are right when they
say that the modern picture of our place in the universe is deeply
alarming. Having lost the old sustaining and guiding framework
that formerly gave meaning to our lives we feel that we are in a
void, with no idea of what to make of ourselves. We shudder at
the thought of our transience and our aloneness.

At this point, when religion as surrounding protective doctrinal
framework has passed away, we find that religion as spirituality
is more than ever relevant. It is not surprising that in the present
century many people look for guidance more to the old mystics
and spiritual writers than to the old theologians, and that so many
of today's new religious movements are concerned with spirituality and the transformation of consciousness. The old mystics were
relatively indifferent to the external and objective side of religion,

to doctrine and institutions. In many ways they stood where we now stand and faced the questions we now face.

And from the point of view I am now describing, Jesus himself can be seen in a new way. He spoke at a time when many people thought the end of the world was near. The old religious order seemed to be doomed. It trembled and no longer felt secure. People were absurdly preoccupied with the petty concerns and squabbles of daily life, unaware that divine judgment loomed. Jesus' teaching heightened this sense of insecurity and sought to show people the urgent necessity of choosing to assess one's life by an absolute standard that does not pass away, the standard that he called the Kingdom of God. Most people live by merely relative standards, comparing themselves with their neighbours, worrying about who has more prestige, more money, more business; but such a worldly life is futile and anxiety-ridden. Of the world, it passes away with the world. The only way to salvation is by a decision to live one's life by an absolute standard that requires of us singleness of mind, inner integrity and disinterested love.

In this way Jesus can be seen as the basis of a Christian spirituality for today. He states its basic demand and gives to it its orientation. In the past he has been seen as the metaphysical Son of God, founder and guarantor of a great ecclesiastical power-structure and system of doctrine. But that image of him has always seemed, to some at least, to be rather incongruous and today it seems less plausible than ever. On the view I am suggesting Christianity is primarily a way, a path rather than a system of doctrines.

People find it very hard indeed to take this point, because they want the doctrines to be true somehow apart from and independently of the way of life they prescribe for us. But this, radicals say, cannot be so. On the view I am describing, Jesus is a prophet of religious awakening who challenges us to live our lives by an absolute standard. God *is* that standard, which calls us to live the Christian life, which guides us in it and is its goal, a standard which we must choose for ourselves and lay upon ourselves. So God is the guiding principle of the religious life. I understand the meaning of the word God in purely religious terms: what God is is given by the part God plays in the religious life, and that is all. But in most people's minds to have faith is to hold that a colourful and reassuring popular metaphysics is in some way descriptively true, and a theologian's job is to try to convince himself and others that it really *is* true. So he is evaluated not in terms of the merits of his argument or the religious adequacy of his point of view, but in terms of his score against a check-list of doctrines. Yet, as everyone knows, it is quite possible to hold all the orthodox views and not even to have begun to live a Christian life, and in any case in modern times the old dogmatic certainties have been steadily crumbling. The time has now come when our understanding of the faith must be focussed, not around doctrine, but around spirituality and ethics. The security offered by authority and doctrine is in the end illusory; the only final security is that enjoyed by those who have given up the need for security and have learnt to be truly disinterested. Hence on the Christian view the highest fulfilment of our selfhood is selfless love, the mind of a saint.

What then happens to the doctrine, the symbolism, the worship? Religion is social: there has to be a community of faith, and the community must have a common language. This common language is symbolic. Its function is to guide our action and aspiration. It does not describe invisible facts, but shapes the religious life. Thus the church commemorates Christ's death and resurrection by way of reminding itself that we must all die to our old selves and be reborn to a new life, and it affirms Christ's ascension by way of confessing the sovereignty of what he stood for over the way it lives. Thus doctrines should be seen not as metaphysical facts but as spiritual guides, and rituals are not transactions with another world but symbolic ways of expressing our faith and committing ourselves to the way of Christ. On this basis, radicals continue to live in good conscience within the household of faith.

There it is. I promised a plain and stupid sketch, and I have given it.

It sounds so straightforward. Religious meaning can be located now only in the human subject, in the movement of the spiritual life and in the unity of I and Thou, for it is nowhere to be found in the world out there. Out there, there is nothing but the flux, which can be given meaning only by human constructive activity. So it all has to come from within us: that is the upshot of modern anthropocentrism. Accordingly faith must move from heteronomy to autonomy, from being a response to objectively-provided religious meaning to being an active creator of religious meaning. That requires a switch from intellectualism to voluntarism, from faith as a cognitive act to faith as a creative act of the will, positing and pursuing the religious ideal and setting out to realize religious values. Our situation, which in moments when our courage fails looks like one of nihilism, the total collapse of an old world of objectively and traditionally given meanings and values, can also be seen in our better moments as one of extraordinary freedom. We can create the world we want, so we must create the best world. The symbol of the Kingdom of God signifies an age in which the sacred is fully internalized within people and coincides with their creativity and freedom; and was it not always true that Christianity is not something that is inherited, for you are not born a Christian but must *choose* to become one? Christianity is not the past, not tradition, not the old world; for it really is an eschatological faith, a new life voluntarily embarked upon by single individuals who have wholly renounced the old world. The sacrament of baptism says just what I am saying here. As for modern Christian agnosticism, well, the Victorians invented 'agnosticism' in the belief that it was an alternative to faith; but the church had rejected metaphysical gnosis and taught its own *agnōsia* seventeen centuries earlier. Christian agnosticism had the function of maintaining in its full purity and strenuousness the demand of faith upon the will. Active love for the neighbour and active pursuit of the 'secret discipline' were not to be enervated by any belief in short cuts.

It sounds so simple – but it is not. My bland and banal account has left out the hard thing, the message that cannot be understood, which is just how deep you have to go into the Void before you can make the transition to Hyperborean faith. Nobody wants to know about *that*. We may be willing to recognize in theory that the centre of Christianity is a moment of dereliction, loss, tragedy, emptiness, meaninglessness; but we cherish the hope that Christ went into the Void in order to spare us the necessity of doing so, rather than to show us the necessity of doing so; and we like to think that the Resurrection reverses the Cross and brings back the old order, the old God, the old life. But, says Hegel,[43] following a hint from Luther, the old God died on the cross permanently and the new life begins on the far side of that loss. In the new life God is not claimed to be more than a guiding principle, an ideal, or (poetically) a Spirit within. Thus to break through to the Hyperborean faith that I am describing really *is* to lose faith, to go through the deepest nihilism until we have learnt that there is no other possibility but to create faith, to make believe, on the far side of the loss of faith.

To those who stick rigorously within the limits of thought, accepting the limitations of our humanity and the purely prescriptive and action-guiding character of religious beliefs, and not allowing themselves to be deceived, the Void can become the Ineffable and can arouse (non-cognitive) worship. But the standing temptation is to project a picture upon the Void, and then to trick oneself into forgetting that it is after all only a projection, and lean on it for comfort. So many people do this, especially those who in the latter half – or more likely, the last decade – of their lives suddenly wake up to their own neglect of religion and begin a desperate religious quest. The Void did not trouble them when they were young and absorbed in life, but now as life slips away they see the Void coming and they are terrified by it. So they fall back on the theological realism of childhood. There must be something out there, and they want some experience or some authority to restore objectivity, for they believe that salvation lies in making contact with Something apart from us and greater than us which can console us. In this way they become easy prey for deceivers and self-deception of every kind. From their starting-point there is only the Void and the pictures we ourselves paint on it. Every Something-out-there that they claim to find is only a picture that they have painted for themselves, their fingers guided by some authoritative hand that they have persuaded themselves to trust.

It can only come from within and it has to come from within, but until we have looked long enough into the Void to feel it turn our bones to water we will not be persuaded. The hard lesson is that since it will not change, we must. To endure the Void we must undergo inner transformation, learn a discipline of selflessness, purge the terror of the Void by renouncing that in ourselves which it terrifies. Then, and not before, will it become the Ineffable.

4

CHRIST (I): GATHERING UP THE FRAGMENTS

Historical change brings about mysterious shifts in the boundaries of the believable, and changes the shapes of the great questions of life. Such a shift has quite recently brought about an odd process of disintegration. Religious thought used to revolve about certain great unifying symbols that had the power to gather up and knit together all the different aspects of our experience, but in the modern period, as our various principal ways of thinking have fanned out and become more clearly differentiated from each other, we have come to a point where our experience resists any comprehensive unification. The integrating symbols have weakened, the world has fallen apart and the ancient mythic feeling for an ultimate unity is gone, but yet — and this is the important realization — we find that many of the component parts of the old integrating symbols do still remain with us and can be put to constructive use. The systematic unity is lost, but the believer can and must make a life out of what Kierkegaard might have called 'untheological fragments'. I'll go further: we will find in the end that the fragments add up to more than the primitive unity out of which they were broken.

The prime case is God. To the ordinary person God was once an almighty, invisible super-person out there, the beginning and end of all things, who controlled all aspects of experience and to whom all things could be referred. To put it more exactly, belief in God had a metaphysical core that held it together. God was the coping-stone, the Most-Real Being, a world-transcending infinite Spirit beyond space and time and yet everywhere present and active in his unbounded power, wisdom and goodness; the

ontological source and goal of all. In himself God was absolutely
simple, the still centre of the turning world, but his outworkings
extended to all aspects and every detail of the manifold and
changing cosmos.

For this account to be socially effective and intellectually
convincing, the culture in which it is held must itself be coherent
enough to be capable of unification, and the available religious
symbols have to be strong enough to encompass, appropriate and
transform all the different aspects of experience. There has to be
a world that is unifiable, and there have to be symbols to unify it.
Such a world we no longer have. To quote just one example, the
old well-loved biblical creation story wove into a single account
the origins of the universe, the evolution of life, the emergence of
mankind, and the foundation of the moral and religious order;
but the best creation-story available today, that offered by modern
physical cosmology, has nothing at all to do with society or ethics.
Where once there was a single sacred story, there is now a whole
series of distinct sciences and ways of thinking. Multiply such
examples, and one begins to see that modern culture has become
a loose assemblage of disparate and largely autonomous conversations. So far as anything still holds them together, it is not
religious myth but man and language. Each of the many discourses
is in continual change and may at a particular moment be more or
less coherent internally, but they do not all add up, they refuse to
be fitted together to make a unified sacred totality. The process of
disintegration began over three centuries ago, and it is now so far
advanced that even among those who have resisted it most fiercely
many are willing to concede privately that the centre cannot hold
much longer.

Yet even after the old unifying vision has gone, many of the
constituents of the older faith in God remain, untheological
fragments that can still be put to use. There are three in particular;
we might call them the Ineffable, the Ideal, and the mythic Person.

First there is God as the Ineffable, the mystery of existence. To
be aware of the limits of language and of the fragmentary and
man-centred character of our apprehension of the world is to be
aware indirectly of an immense unknowable mystery that surrounds our life. The best and most disciplined souls resist the
temptation to paint the Ineffable with archaic colours or to project
human fantasies upon it, yet they may well spend a lifetime

meditating upon it, without such a life being wasted. The Belgian painter René Magritte was such a man. He was an austere spirit, strangely at home in our modern Ice Age. He liked to say, 'There is a mystery in the universe, but what is it?'[1] He said that his paintings were intended to evoke the mystery of the universe,[2] but he is so cool that these works can hardly be called religious in the traditional sentimental and anthropomorphic sense. Magritte seeks no guidance or consolation whatsoever. He seeks only to articulate as clearly and precisely as he can his sense of the ineffable mystery of the world. Again, to take a very different character who was also a painter, Claude Monet began as a fairly commonplace artist, but through long years of intense dedication and high productivity he eventually worked his way to mastery, a purely objective and selfless delight in the flux of experience and the play of light upon plants and water. Such men as these display a kind of sanctity. Magritte read much philosophy and liked puzzles, whereas Monet, who was less obviously intellectual, achieved in the end something like a Buddhist vision of landscape. But in their different ways they both show very clearly one element in traditional belief in God, an attentive cosmic wonder; and they show it in a singularly purified form which has become quite detached from the other elements of religious belief and now exists on its own.

It is worth digressing briefly here to notice that many modern painters have shown very clearly the spiritual significance of what is too often described disparagingly as 'reductionism'. No major abstract painter began as a abstract painter. They all developed towards abstraction. Piet Mondrian, for example, began by working in the manner of Van Gogh and Cezanne and moved through cubism to geometrical abstraction and then, at his furthest extreme, to minimalism. This development coincided with the changeover from an epoch in which biology and history were the most influential sciences to an age in which mathematical physics were perceived as the most beautiful and highly-developed science. In the finest religious spirits of the period one can detect a corresponding shift from a preoccupation with the historical, developing and institutional side of religion towards a personal search for inner purity and integrity. Mondrian himself was strongly influenced by a form of Protestantism,[3] and the best abstract paintings by him and others have often been seen as icons of religious minimalism. They express a deep conviction that in the twentieth century, and indeed for the foreseeable future, we need to find out how light we can travel; we need to learn a kind of Buddhist inner simplicity and even emptiness. For many this quest has been very demanding, as we are poignantly reminded when we look with his suicide in mind at Rothko's glowing late masterpieces, or when we recall the end of Simone Weil. But the quest has been necessary, and still is, and it is a serious mistake to dismiss it as reductionism, as if we all somehow knew reductionism to be a bad thing. On the contrary, in religion reductionism is called the Purgative Way, and it is essential.

To return: there is, secondly, God the religious Ideal, the guiding principle and goal of the religious life. In mystical writers such as Eckhart and St John of the Cross the various things that are said of God function as regulative principles that prescribe the structure of the spiritual life and point to its goal. Thus God can be demythologized into spirituality;[4] for whereas mythical thinking projects God out and personifies him, mystical thinking works in the opposite direction, seeing God as internal to the spiritual life, his metaphysical attributes representing the way the demands of such a life bear upon us and his moral attributes representing various aspects of its goal. There is nothing arbitrary in this, for just as to acknowledge an artistic vocation is *eo ipso* to accept the demands imposed upon one by the choice of a life dedicated to art, so also to acknowledge a religious vocation is simply to choose and accept the requirements of the religious life. The two cases are pretty close to each other: the artist may speak of what his Muse requires of him, and the religious man of what God requires. Nothing metaphysical need be implied by this way of speaking of God. It is logically distinct both from the sense of cosmic wonder and from any postulated need to live by myths and personifications. All we are saying is that this way of speaking about God is a way of pointing out what as a matter of fact are the requirements of a way of life that aims at spiritual perfection.

Thirdly, there is God the myth, the God of the ordinary person's piety, God experienced as an invisible heavenly Person who is both over against us and within us. This God is experienced as a heavenly Father or compassionate Lord. The moral life is interpreted as being lived under his eye and is motivated by a desire to please him by doing his will. His help is sought and found in the daily business of life, and prayer is practised and experienced as personal communion with him. It may help to remove misunderstanding if I make it clear that I in no way question the subjective vividness and moral force of this way of experiencing God; but at the same time truthfulness compels us to point out that it is highly specific to particular religious communities and is in fact socially determined. The personal God is tied rigorously to the study of a particular set of scriptures, particular religious practices, and life as a member of a particular religious community. The people who do these things and who comprise this society know their god by this particular name as their personal God. In former times, when society was more homogeneous, when one particular religious system was culturally dominant and when people lacked the concept of myth, then experience of this personal God was so general and powerful that he became in effect public and objectively real. He was the foundation of the whole social order, and talk of him had a wide range of publicly-accepted explanatory uses. But the cultural changes that have taken place since those days oblige us now to put the matter rather differently. The reason why the personal God is so highly specific, the reason why (in the old language) he is convenanted to a particular community, is that he is actually created by the apparatus of a particular religion, and his vivid reality to the believer manifests the almost boundless power of society to evoke and to shape the inner experience of the individual. So I have to be aware that my personal God is the expression and the vehicle of the faith of my religious community. There is a Jewish God, a Muslim God, a Russian God, and so on. But to acknowledge this is not in any way to impugn either the need for community in religion or the value and the reality of the personal God for the believer, for the personal God of practical religion is indeed a valuable vehicle for building up group religious life and feeling and for enabling ordinary people to enter upon and participate in the spiritual life.

The ineffable mystery that surrounds our life, the structure and claims of the spiritual path, and the personal God of everyday practical religion – these are three fragments of the old comprehensive faith in God that have survived the death of God. What has been lost is the old naive ontology that used to synthesize them and so enabled people to see the Ineffable as a transcendent Being, the spiritual life as having an objective ontological goal, and the ecclesiastical-mythical experience of a personal God as being straightforwardly cognitive. The three components used to converge and be held together metaphysically. The philosopher and the common man could both be realists or 'literal' theists. But when we come to understand that *all* our notions of what is really out there are just provisional human constructions, then we see that our age unavoidably lacks any such unifying metaphysical vision. We have only the fragments; but as I have indicated, there is still quite enough left for us to live by.

Something similar has happened in the case of Christ. He also used to be a transcendent individual person, the God-man who was none other than Jesus of Nazareth, who was also the archetype and exemplar of the principle of death and rebirth in the spiritual life, and who was also the great ecclesiastical-mythical figure who symbolized ideal human perfection and sovereignty in a hominized cosmos. All these different facets of Christ-talk were felt to cohere in a single individual person, but today they have fallen apart. We still have the constituents, historical, spiritual and mythical, but we no longer have the ontological principle that once held them together.

In the case of God, the unifying principle was removed when transcendent or dogmatic metaphysics was overthrown by Hume and Kant in the eighteenth century. Since their time, all accounts of God that deserve serious consideration have been in some degree revisionist. In the case of Christ the story has been rather more complex. Criticism of the belief that human beings can have knowledge of a transcendent invisible personal companion has been extended from the case of God to the case of Christ, and the study of other religions has shown that the various moments and structures in the spiritual life which for Christians are embodied in the person of Christ are also paralleled in other faiths that do not know his name. But the most influential factor has no doubt been biblical criticism. D. F. Strauss and others grasped that the historical Jesus, the Jewish teacher, was a very different figure from the transcendent Christ of faith[5] who is represented in the great cycle of christological doctrines and festivals; and once that distinction had been clearly made, the way was open for it to be said that the Christ of faith was a mythic figure. A realist view of the Christ of faith, as an identifiable real person out there, depended upon the possibility of identifying him as being none other than Jesus of Nazareth risen from the dead. That confidence was lost when it became clear both that the Christ of faith has been a historically-conditioned and very variable figure, and that the original Jesus is a very much fainter and stranger figure than had hitherto been supposed.

It is true that the historical momentum of Christian language has rolled on to the present day and has ensured that a great deal of highly realistic talk about Christ can still be heard. Catholics may speak of Christ as being 'really present' in the elements or the action of the Eucharist. But such language is clearly metaphorical. Some may say Christ's body and blood are really present in the elements of the Eucharist, and others that his person is really present in its action; but in both cases it has to be admitted that the ordinary secular criteria for the presence of blood or of a person are not satisfied. What can be meant by the use of such language? – Only, that the Eucharist is a ritual way of binding ourselves to the Christian life, committing ourselves to that group of values and principles to live by which is to live in Christ. Analytically, Christ is present where his followers gather 'in his Name', and celebrate in his memory the victory of his love. Again, evangelical Christians speak of the exalted Jesus as being in a descriptive or 'literal' sense their invisible superhuman friend and companion, whom they really 'know', who accompanies them constantly, listens to them, speaks to them and dwells in their hearts. Their experience of him becomes so real to them that they admit to no doubt that they know what they mean in speaking as they do. Yet in so speaking they strain language far beyond any possibility of descriptive meaning, and their rigid refusal to admit that they are using language in a strange and unnatural way gives rise to doubts about the usefulness of continuing the conversation.

For what can it mean to claim that an invisible person walks with me, that I know him, that he accompanies me, that he exercises a transforming influence upon me, and that he indwells me? In secular contexts such claims are nowadays taken as evidence of insanity, as in a recent murder trial where the defence tried to prove that the defendant was in the grip of such ideas in order to persuade the court that he was unfit to plead. Our continuing tolerance of such language in religious contexts must be due partly to our regarding it as a hallowed survival of earlier ways of thinking, and partly to the fact that in practice we

nowadays interpret it metaphorically. In former days people
certainly did believe in spirit-agency and spirit-possession, but
today belief in spirit-agency has no remaining explanatory value
in secular contexts, and there is no secular case – except perhaps
in psychopathology – where we speak in a fully realistic sense of
one person as indwelling another. The result is that traditional
realistic talk of Christ's invisible supernatural presence and activity has entirely lost the cultural context within which it could
appear to have descriptive force; and that is why naive attempts
to intrude such language into modern conversations seem eccentric and cause embarrassment. Insofar as believers still use realistic
language, they do so by a *tour de force* by which they bear
eloquent witness to the power over them of the group to which
they belong. Thinking he is bearing witness to Christ, the twice-
born believer in fact merely exhibits the strange and sinister power
of the group over him, the group which puts him under such very
great psychological pressure to testify that he is enjoying certain
experiences and to speak of them in certain authorized formulae.
From a philosophical point of view we must conclude that if
someone claims that a dead person lives in his heart and wields
influence over him, then the life must be metaphorical and the
influence moral. To admit this is to see a chance to achieve
something which many people are seeking (though they do not
usually care to put it quite so bluntly), namely a way of reconciling
faith with sanity.

The implications for christology are non-realist. The realist
believer, in some cases at least, experienced Christ as a real
invisible person with whom he was acquainted and whose influence he experienced. This invisible person he identified with the
Jesus of the Gospels, the identification being sustained by study of
the scriptures and by the authority of the church and her sacraments. Thus the unifying principle of christology, the Christ of
faith, was a real supernatural person who was personally identical
with Jesus of Nazareth, who was active in the rites of the church
and who was identifiable in religious experience.

It is characteristic of pre-critical thinking that people within it
are unaware of how far such a system of ideas is circular and
systematically self-confirming. Religious authority and the religious symbol-system, when internalized within the believer, work
so powerfully to structure his thinking that he truly seems to

himself to be having experiences that confirm the truth of his faith. All was well, and the circle remained unbroken, until in the nineteenth century the identification of the Christ of faith with Jesus began to come apart. Once the Christ of faith had lost his external historical grounding in Jesus, in an event-resurrection and in Jesus' guarantees to the church, then it could be seen that he, the Christ of faith, is an ecclesiastical-mythical construction of the same kind as the Blessed Virgin Mary, though of higher rank in the system. Catholic Modernism was a courageous theological movement that attempted to become conscious of this truth within the context of a continuing commitment to the Roman Catholic faith. It was suppressed, yet any historian of art or piety knows that the Christ of faith has evolved historically, and has over the centuries been far too many disparate things for them all to be securely grounded in the Jesus of history.

The upshot of this discussion is that a unified systematic 'christology' of the old kind cannot now be written, even though many people naturally still make the attempt. The different aspects of Christ were synthesized on the basis of a confidence in the historicity of the Gospels (especially St John's Gospel) and in the reality of invisible spirit-beings acting upon us, which can no longer be justified. All the footnotes and all the learning in the world cannot change this situation, nor is there in the long run anything to be gained either by fudging the issues or by shooting the messenger who brings the bad news. It is best to be truthful and to say that even though we cannot synthesize them, certain substantial fragments of the old christology do remain to us. They are three in number, and they correspond to the three fragments of the old belief in God. To God as the Ineffable corresponds the historical Jesus: I shall argue that we can still trace to him and associate with his name a certain use of irony to bring about religious awakening, a small but all-important shift in consciousness. To God as the guiding Ideal of the spiritual life corresponds the dying and rising Jesus as a symbol of rebirth and of the principle of loss and gain in the spiritual life. Finally, to God the Father, the mythic Person of ecclesiastically-moulded faith, there corresponds the fully-mythicized Christ of faith who is shown forth to the faithful in the great cycle of doctrines and festivals, and who represents the promise of a renewal and liberation of humanity through the Christian movement.

The structural analogy between the two cases is fascinating and subtle, but it is important not to be seduced by it into an attempt to restore the old unities in new forms. We can do better than that.

5

CHRIST (II): THE IRONIST

Interpretations of Jesus are so diverse that anyone who considers all of them can scarcely avoid concluding that it must be well-nigh impossible to show that just one of them is correct. In particular discussions we usually find that the problem has been simplified by a tacit agreement between writer and reader to exclude most of the interpretations from serious consideration, and attend only to that limited range of options which among 'us' is understood to be respectable. Looked at from an uncommitted and purely rational point of view, religious issues are so sprawling and diffuse that people feel the need of a little political pressure to reduce them to manageable proportions. So for Jewish, for Christian or for Muslim writers, there is in each case a more-or-less standard interpretation of Jesus. He is seen as an original freelance teacher from the rabbinic golden age, as Israel's promised Messiah, the universal saviour and Word of God incarnate, or as the last great prophet before Muhammad; and in each case there is a certain permitted latitude of interpretation on either side of the standard view. Other views are set aside as being out of the question, or are rejected by the political device of labelling them irresponsible – and so the issues are kept under control. Rationality is relative to a particular community's assumptions and interests. Yet not only are there these three major communally-held interpretations of Jesus, but also he has been seen with some plausibility, both in ancient and modern times, as a folk-magician, as a gnostic teacher-redeemer and as a political revolutionary. In addition, a thin line of modern writers has regarded him as an almost wholly mythical figure. Some have pushed his dates back several genera-

tions to identify him with the mysterious teacher who inspired the
Qumran community, and there has even been an attempt to
advance his dates in order to identify him with Jesus the son of
Ananias, described by Josephus as having prophesied against the
Temple during the 60s.

Awareness both of the full range of options, and of the devices
used to limit the threat their variety presents, makes one increasingly cautious. Until a few years ago I held that the main outlines
of Jesus' career and message could be reconstructed with high
probability, basically by stripping away the superimposed Christian ideas from the accounts of him given by Mark and in the
material common to Matthew and Luke. Underneath, I thought,
there was a credible picture of a Jewish teacher. Then I moved to
a more cautious position, accepting only the barest outline bi-
ography of him that is attested by Paul and other New Testament
writers outside the Gospels, and with regard to his teaching
admitting that we have no way of singling out any original and
unretouched sayings, but claiming nevertheless that behind the
core-tradition of parables and sayings there is still to be heard a
distinctive voice using special rhetorical techniques for bringing
about religious awakening in his hearers. Now, even that seems
too bold. It is better to say that when we study a figure from an
exotic and pre-modern culture who has left us no writings in his
own hand, we cannot expect to be able to intuit his unique
personal individuality without the risk of back-projection and
fantasy. Jesus is now a figure like Socrates. The name is not so
much the name of a distinctly-graspable individual human being
as rather the name of something that appeared at a certain decisive
moment in human history, a little shift in consciousness that
changed things permanently, something that can still be specified
even though its precise grounding in a particular individual can
no longer be discerned.

So considered, the name Socrates designates the source of a
particular intellectual tradition, and the name Jesus designates the
one who introduced a certain form of religious awareness. Both
were consciousness-raisers. Socrates used a questioning irony in
order to create in his hearers just a little internal distancing,
enough to make them pause and wonder if they really understood
the meanings of the words they were using. That wonder is
philosophy, and simply by using a few linguistic techniques to

evoke it Socrates made a permanent difference to human consciousness. His name is the name of a small quantum-jump in thinking, and that is enough.

Jesus, I shall argue, was also an ironist. He appears to have used parables and reversal-sayings – the construction is technically called 'antithetic parallelism'[1] – with an ironical intention, to create a little internal distancing within the self which makes it possible to appraise one's own relation to existence from a new point of view.

The cultural context which Jesus shared and within which he expressed his message was a vivid expectation of the imminent end of all things. The whole frame of reference within which men ordinarily see their lives was about to disappear. That meant that our customary ways of thinking, by which we derive from the world the standards by which we assess the way we live and what we are, are becoming obsolete and absurd. They break down; they fail us. Our way of living, our whole world, even our very existence is in question. What is one to be and to do, how is one to assess things in the face of the unthinkable, when everything passes away? Jesus uses irony in order to prise people apart a little from themselves, distancing them just sufficiently from their instinctive clinging to the old self and the old world for them to be able to glimpse the possibility of choosing something altogether new. What that new thing is cannot be said directly, but irony is suitably indirect. It introduces a second and contrasting value-scale, but it does so in a cunning, surreptitious and half-concealed way. You have to be in the know in order to be able to detect its presence. It is easily missed if you do not have ears to hear.

The name of Jesus, then, now signifies a moment of religious awakening by the use of irony. I shall assign to irony a much higher religious value than it has been given before, even by Kierkegaard, whose principal discussion of the subject was unfortunately written too early in his authorship.[2] It has tended to commit him, and has certainly committed his interpreters, to too low a view of irony. On the whole the young Kierkegaard saw irony as Aristophanes saw Socrates – suspended in a basket between earth and heaven.[3] Irony, says Kierkegaard, raises you up far enough above the unthinking bustle of life for you to be able to perceive its absurdity, but not far enough for you to be able to reach heaven. Irony's vantage-point exposes the scurrying futility of a way of life shaped by nothing more enduring than transient feelings and fashions, and it may lead you to seek a way of life governed by universal moral principles. But irony does not cut deep enough to shake the soul to its depths, and does not soar high enough to free us from the world altogether and bring us to eternal salvation. For the young Kierkegaard irony's value is only negative and preliminary.

Perhaps the main reason why irony's religious importance has been unrecognized is that it so easily gets a bad name. The stock examples of it carry such strong overtones of dissimulation, malice and conspiracy to mock some hapless victim. For example, suppose that a group of us are gathered about a very minor and very vain poet who is clearly anxious to steer the conversation towards his favourite topic. I may take up that topic, praising his work a shade too highly and giving him a status which in the eyes of all of us except the poet himself is plainly a little excessive. It should be obvious, and I intend it to be obvious to everyone but the poet, that I cannot quite mean what I say, but the unfortunate bard is misled by his own vanity into taking me at face value. He preens himself, and we briefly catch each other's eyes in a secret smile at his expense.

Irony in this case has not been used in a good way, to open up a new possibility of self-knowledge, but in a malicious way, to expose the lack of it. The more delicate the irony, the meaner the trick that is played and the better the joke, for the joke consists in our pleasure at finding ourselves joined together in a transient, featherlight conspiracy of mutual understanding which has united us by excluding our victim. The irony must isolate the victim, keep him in the dark, and create a small amused confederacy of people who are in the know.

Again, consider how when meeting a loudmouth I may affect a most earnest and sincere deference and beg to be instructed by him. So I lure him forward into making a fool of himself. This time the joke is that the victim digs his own grave as, all unawares, he blunderingly widens the gulf between his own self-estimation and the quite contrary opinion that the rest of us have of him.

There is worse to come, for through these exercises we have learnt something of the dialectics of power-relationships in human groups. A bullied schoolboy learns that the best way to avoid being made a fool is to play the fool, and embarks upon a career of currying favour by self-vilification, a career that may in some cases end in his becoming one of the strangest and saddest of human figures, the kind of popular comedian whom we pay handsomely to lacerate himself for our pleasure. In a more modest way, most of us learn to win favour – or at least, to avoid being made fools of – by being ironical at our own expense. This is reckoned a decent thing to do, but is such mild self-disparagement sincere or not? If it is sincerely meant, then by rating ourselves too low we avoid giving ourselves to life as we should; but if it is insincere, then it seems to be nothing but a form of inverted boasting. And if, as is nearer the mark, irony cannot appropriately be categorized as being either sincere or otherwise, then what becomes of its morality?

Again, in dramatic irony the stage character's blissful ignorance of his real situation and unpleasant prospects gives us malicious satisfaction. And when we speak of an irony of fate or an ironical outcome of events we mean that the way the world runs is often as malicious as we are ourselves. What fate has in store for people is often cruelly enlightening or bitterly appropriate.

No wonder irony gets a bad name, when it is so often used to gratify the worst in human nature. Instead of being used as a consciousness-raising tool, it is very commonly employed to make fools of people by showing them up before others as not being in the know, and then prolonging the joke by keeping the victim in the dark as long as possible. In *Twelfth Night* his tormentors can only continue speaking ironically to Malvolio so long as he remains unaware of what is going on. The game is that everything said to Malvolio must have two meanings, one for him in the dark and another for the rest of us who are in the know. Truly virtuous and religious people reject cruelty and duplicity in any form, and when Olivia finds out what has been happening she puts a stop to it at once. So it seems natural to conclude that moral goodness and religious seriousness preclude irony. The ironist's wit is merely sophisticated heartlessness, and his command of the situation is based on double-mindedness and insincerity. Be good, sweet maid, and let who will be clever.

From this moral rejection of irony it is but a short step to those movements in literature and religion that have attempted to overcome the ironical spirit and banish it completely. Wordsworth and Lawrence are examples of writers who sought to recover the truth of immediate feeling and teach us to live from the heart, and the Pietistic and Evangelical movements have attempted something similar in religion. In both cases there was a revolt against rationalism, cynicism and heartless urban wit and an attempt to restore simple directness and whole-heartedness. To do this it was necessary to disregard the obvious charges of naivety and sentimentality, because the whole aim was to overcome the inwardly-divided and ungenerous mentality from which such charges emanate. If the double-minded spirit, critical and self-critical, mocking and self-mocking, were allowed any foothold at all, it would once more insinuate itself to poison the wells of feeling and weaken our commitment to life. So both writers and men of religion could think it fitting and even necessary to be uncritical in their praise of joyous innocence and childlike faith, simplicity and trustfulness.

The tendency in all this towards an outright rejection of self-awareness is encouraged by the close affinity in the English language between consciousness and conscience, self-knowledge and self-reproach. Especially in the English tradition, we are often *most* conscious when we blush because the turn of events has made our true motives more nakedly apparent than we would wish, and *least* conscious when 'lost' in admiration. It is as if self-consciousness always brings bad news, and as if the highest aesthetic and religious states of the soul are always unconscious; as if whenever the conscious and critical aspect of the self is roused into activity it always find something to be pained about. It not only passes moral judgment upon the affective aspect of the self, but also finds it positively embarrassing. So it keeps it hidden as if it were something shameful, and allows it only jesting or ironical expression. Anything too nakedly sincere is felt to be a social *faux pas* that makes us blush. But this, say our neo-puritans, is absurd. When self-knowledge makes us chronically and morbidly embarrassed by ourselves, and so threatens personal integrity as to make any whole-hearted response impossible, we are better off without it. Habitual irony at one's own expense seems to be as cruel and double-minded a business as habitual irony at other people's expense.

All this makes it clear enough why irony can lose friends and why many people reject, or at least see no special religious value in, the critical, self-conscious and ironical spirit. But what of religion without irony? Many of today's religious movements are strongly anti-intellectual, but it can scarcely be claimed that the result is a condition of innocence and purity. On the contrary, the kind of religion – sprouting up everywhere today – which is anti-intellectual, and has no self-criticism and no saving sense of its own absurdity, is all too often arrogant, bigoted, self-deceived and self-regarding. Its every prejudice is a divine inspiration and its doctrines are maintained with an obtuse literalness which kills the spirit. The ordinary person rightly regards it as a psychological trap, a kind of madness. When he hears that a serious commitment to religion requires that we should voluntarily run ourselves into that trap, and then block our own chances of escaping from it by strapping ourselves in with the many and familiar devices that are all-too-generously provided by every religious group, then he rightly recoils in horror. Almost all new religious movements nowadays have an air of brainwashing about them. Jesus' once-beautiful saying that the gospel is for the sick is acquiring a very sinister ring in an age whose typical religious movements are so often little more than waves of mass psychosis.

The attempt to repress the modern critical and ironical consciousness and revert to an allegedly more innocent condition, locked dogmatically into a myth with no possibility of transcending it, is a disaster. Today, true religion has to be ironical, combining a full commitment to religious ideals with the consciousness, the freedom and the sense of absurdity that irony gives. How is this possible, and what might be a truly religious interpretation of irony?

Irony rests on a perception of incongruity between the human subject and some independent circumstance or point of view which threatens his customary assessment of himself. For much of the time we are not seriously disturbed in our self-possession and our confidence that we know what we are driving at. Our self-estimation and our sense of the meaning of our own action are not seriously challenged. The world about us seems to take us at face value, and our words and deeds fit in with, and are taken up into, the general stream of life. There is not a significant gap between what we think we are up to and what others take us to be up to. Now and again, though, it can happen that there is a curious breakdown when, as people say, it suddenly becomes apparent that we have got hold of the wrong end of the stick or are barking up the wrong tree. Perhaps through simple and pardonable ignorance of some relevant fact, we have formed an entirely mistaken picture of the situation. We have sized things up wrongly. What we say or do misfires badly and fails to accomplish anything, and for a while we are utterly at a loss.

How does this come about? In order to engage normally with life we have to pick up the thread of what is going on; that is, we have to set up an internal framework of understanding in terms of which we can interpret what is happening and frame our own actions accordingly. On a small scale, we can see this being done when a newcomer joins a group at a party and tries to pick up the thread so that he can contribute to the talk. Watch the eyes flicker from one face to another, searching for tiny clues. The quicker he can get the hang of things and intervene with an apposite remark the better. He shows that he belongs and is part of the group. Speed of this kind, being quick on the uptake, is remarkably popular and causes a curious glow of pleasure all round. Why? — Because society at large lives by and depends upon a rich and complex network of shared understandings and sympathies, and we are always very pleased to learn that this deep consensus is in good condition. But there is always the possibility that the newcomer's remark may fail to connect, and when that happens it has a very depressing effect on everyone's spirits. It is a lead balloon.

It is a very unsettling and sceptical thought that at any moment the framework of understanding in terms of which we are living may suddenly and quite unpredictably fail us through no fault of our own. Many existentialist and other philosophers have claimed that it lies entirely within our own power to guarantee the meaningfulness of our own lives, but evidently they are mistaken. The absurd cannot be held off in that way, for it is perfectly possible for a sane and sober person to seem to himself to be quite *au fait*, while yet there are circumstances unknown to him in the light of which his words and deeds are meaningless nonsense.

An ironical awareness is, then, an awareness that all our frameworks of understanding are merely human and can never be trusted absolutely. People who live within a single supernaturally-guaranteed framework naturally see no need for irony. For them one view of things is secure. Taking it that their framework is objectively founded, they hold as a matter of faith that it simply must be unfalsifiable and proof against all threats. And so in a sense it is, for *they themselves make it so*. The community has thoughtfully equipped them with 'blocks to falsifiability', devices for explaining away any counter-evidence that may crop up. They seize on these devices gratefully and use them readily to defend the framework against criticism, but they must do it unconsciously so as not to become aware that their cherished 'objectivity' is nothing but a socially-created and socially-maintained illusion. There is unhappily no way in which they can learn how deeply they deceive themselves. But when we as observers grasp how they do the trick and how the illusion maintains itself, then we ourselves become critical. We realize that all frameworks of understanding are human constructions and none is objectively secured against collapse. Thus our conscious-ness becomes ironical through and through. We cannot avoid being both committed and detached, living by a belief-system while at the same time sitting light to it. Self-knowledge now takes the form of awareness of our own radical vulnerability, and all dogmatism breaks down.

It is noticeable that the loss of a framework of understanding is an advance in self-knowledge. Loss is gain; but that does not make the losing any less painful. Oedipus in Sophocles' play does not merely lack a piece of information; he lacks self-knowledge. He does not wish to know the truth, even when it is staring him in the face. He reaches a point where he is desperately clinging to an indefensible self-understanding because he still cannot bear the terrible truth, even when it is becoming more and more obvious. Indeed, the closer the truth comes, the more he dreads and resists it.

At such a moment it may be the teacher's work to be cruel to be kind, by administering the *coup de grâce*. He uses irony in speaking to a person who is so locked into a false and illusory self-understanding that he cannot be told the truth directly. He is not in the way of truth at all. Only irony can get past his defences and lead him stumbling out towards self-exposure and self-know-ledge. Thus it was that Socrates used an indirect or reverse method in order to overcome people's resistance to the truth, like a wrestler who throws an opponent by drawing out and then deflecting the opponent's own strength.

Although the teacher's intentions are merciful in such a case, the pain of coming to oneself is great and the teacher will inevitably be blamed for it. Poetically, it is fitting that he should be a martyr. The more profound the healing he brings, the more pain he causes and the more resentment he brings down upon his own head. It is in this sense that Jesus voluntarily died for our sins.

For Jesus' use of irony is, if anything, even more thoroughgoing than that of Socrates. His audience are people who for most of the time see nothing wrong with their own self-estimation and their own worldly scale of values. Like everyone else they are busy with their own affairs, buying and selling, getting and spending, marrying and giving in marriage; and what is wrong with that? But there is just one little thing they have forgotten – the coming of God. Take *that* into account, and their self-important little world collapses into meaninglessness.

Socrates' irony has a philosophical purpose. Since we will not be able really to learn anything until we have first learnt to question everything we ordinarily take unthinkingly for granted, be begins by undermining people's self-assurance and forcing them to question their knowledge. What sets Jesus' irony in motion is the way the arrival of divine judgment shows up the absurdity of all ordinary human valuations. Usually we are like the people in Jesus' parables, preoccupied with worldly relativities, comparing ourselves with each other, asking who is being paid more, who is doing better, who deserves more, who has higher status and what is of higher price. But Jesus is intensely aware of the looming Abyss, and his preaching is ironical because he has so clear a sense of an absolute standard in the light of which all these relative judgments suddenly look foolish. The divine judgment upon us is simply the final truth about us; it is how we appear from a standpoint which knows all and misses nothing. The extent to which it comes as an annihilating shock is the measure of our alienation from the truth about ourselves. Hence Jesus' irony is strongly satirical in tone:[4] a person who cannot find his spectacles because they are on his nose may be comical enough, but a person who has forgotten *himself* is the ultimate absurdity. Yet in the world as it is this condition of ultimate absurdity is what passes for normality!

Irony is liberating when it has, not the duplicity of some secular irony, but the agreeable amphibiousness of the religious outlook. It shows us how there can be, unknown to us, a point of view

which knows us better than we know ourselves and therefore has
the power to unmake and remake us. Irony is a revelatory tool
which opens the way to the religious life.

It would be going too far to claim that our spelling-out of the
religious significance of irony is a true exegesis of the message of
the historical Jesus, because we know too little of him, and because
in any case the very idea of a true exegesis for today of a distant
historical figure is so highly contentious. But at least it can be said
that the sense of a collision between two different orders of things,
two scales of values of which one is obvious and the other
mysterious or hidden, is central to the Gospels and has in many
different forms remained in Christianity throughout its history.
Consider, for example, the contrasts between the old and the new,
law and gospel, justice and love, reason and ecstasy, institutional
order and radical freedom, nature and grace, king and prophet,
state and church, world-affirmation and world-denial, things
temporal and things eternal, the mediated and the immediate,
discursive and intuitive reason, and finally the holy contrasted
with the profane versus the holy identified with the profane.
Christianity has always drawn its peculiar restless energy from
such contrasts as these, and has seen their source in Jesus.
Poetically at least, the figure in the Gospels presents in a highly-
condensed form the whole range of Christianity's subsequent
unfolding spiritual life.

However, if religious awakening depends upon an ironical
perception of incongruity and opposition, then Christianity cannot be content simply to accept without question the reconciling,
validatory, cosmological and civilization-defending task that is
always thrust upon it by the political Right. Conservative pessimism looks back in anguish to the Middle Ages as the period when
the two orders were most nearly synthesized, and sees all our
cultural history since then as one of decline and fall. The Reformation and the rise of capitalism broke down the old organic and
hierarchical social order in which everyone knew his place and
introduced a competitive and acquisitive model of human nature;
the rise of modern science broke the links between the moral order
and the natural order; the Enlightenment unleashed a devouring
spirit of autonomous reason which first demythologized everything else and then ended by destroying itself . . . and so the
melancholy catalogue continues, until we talk ourselves into the

mood of romantic pessimism, nostalgia for a lost Eden, existential despair and apocalyptic nihilism which has so often afflicted intellectuals since Nietzsche.

This model of our cultural development is not only dubious as history (supposed golden ages never survive close inspection), but it rests upon a mistaken view of the genius of Christianity. Nietzsche himself largely avoids the fallacy, for he is well aware of at least some of the inner tensions within the Christian tradition.[5] It is not easy to reconcile the ethic of the Kingdom of God with the ethic of any governing class; the will to truth and the demand for inner integrity that is so strong in Christianity has inevitably itself worked to demythologize Christian doctrine from within; and the ethic of universal love and tolerance has always been at odds with the exclusive claims made by the hierarchy in the doctrines that it has defined and imposed upon the church. Nietzsche could see that Christianity is ill-adapted to be a civilization-endorsing faith; but even his insight is imperfect. He was stuck with an image of Christ very like Dostoyevsky's, and never had the chance to consider the implications of a thorough-going eschatological interpretation of Jesus. If he had had that opportunity he might have sensed a further affinity between Jesus' message and his own.

He might also have changed his mind about the religious meaning of the death of God. The God who had died, according to Nietzsche, was the God of classical theism. He had been the ultimate civilization-endorser, providing a single unifying foundation for nature, society and faith. But this objective, cosmological and all-uniting God can scarcely have been the God of Jesus. Even in antiquity there were some – Marcion[6] and certain Christian Gnostics – who had seen that. Jesus' God does not validate the old world and the old order, but rather divides, confounds and destroys in order to free us for a wholly new reality which is yet to come. Of all received Christian assumptions, the hardest to shake is that which identifies the God of objective metaphysical theism with the God of Jesus; but there are great creative possibilities in questioning it.

The argument has moved on by now, and it is too late for conservative nostalgia, too late to suppose that there ever could have been any long-lasting alliance between Christianity and civilization. We have gone too far in the realization that, whatever people have thought to the contrary, human life is always lived on the edge of the Abyss without the support of any objective metaphysical and moral framework, and that pluralism, relativism and scepticism may be kept at bay for a while but can never finally be overcome. It is too late now to claim that our present condition is merely a temporary aberration of the modern West, for which the treason of the clerks makes a most convenient scapegoat. It looks much more as if we are coming to a clearer recognition of what has always been in sober fact the human condition: a sort of permanent eschatological crisis. Beneath the sometimes exotic language in which he speaks of it, it is a condition which Jesus clearly recognizes and to which he speaks: 'How will you choose to live and what will you choose to be, what kind of new human reality will you choose to constitute, when you have fully understood that everything, but *everything*, is passing away?' Jesus may not have been the first to recognize the condition, but he was the first to see in it a stupendous new religious possibility, very close to us.

6

CHRIST (III): THE SAVIOUR

Christians maintain that Jesus Christ is the divine Saviour who by his death on the cross has procured for us the forgiveness of sins. Of all Christian beliefs this is surely the most central and the most deeply moving, but surely also the hardest to understand, to disentangle and to translate into intelligible and credible terms. I believe that a clear and strictly rational interpretation of it can be arrived at, but only after a great deal of dead wood has been hacked away.

Nothing can be achieved merely by quoting texts. Many people still use arguments of the form, 'Jesus said so-and-so, and what Jesus said is true; therefore so-and-so.' Such an argument is, for example, sometimes built around Mark 10.45 ('The Son of Man came . . . to give his life a ransom for many'), this text being as near as the Synoptic Gospels come to teaching a doctrine of the atonement. However, all arguments of this kind depend on the assumptions made in the two premises, that we have some original and unretouched sayings of Jesus and that Jesus is verbally inerrant or infallible. To take the first assumption, if we are ever to substantiate the claim that Jesus really is an historical figure, we must allow the traditions about him to undergo historical criticism; but as soon as historical criticism gets under way, it becomes clear that we can never fully prove that any particular saying is original and unaltered. Comparison of the texts of the Gospels demonstrates that a great many supposed sayings of the Lord have been much revised. Alteration of Jesus' sayings can be proved, whereas that a saying has been transmitted to us quite unaltered can never be proved. As for the second assumption, that Jesus is infallible, this raises the question of Jesus' claims. An enormous amount of attention has been given to this issue, on the basis of an obscure feeling that if it could be shown that Jesus made great claims on his own behalf, then the truth of the great christological dogmas about him would thereby become that bit more probable. The plain man would put it more simply by saying: 'Jesus claimed to be God, therefore Jesus is God.' However, divinity has been claimed by and on behalf of a very large number of historical figures, including a number who are alive today, and even I have met two people who are believed to be gods by substantial numbers of followers. It is clear that the mere making of an impressive claim cannot be sufficient by itself to prove its truth, without the addition of extra premisses. So the argument must be reformulated: 'Jesus claimed to be God; and because we have some independent reasons for believing that his claims are true, therefore he is God.' What could these other reasons be? Some say, the supreme goodness and sanity of Jesus' character; but how do we prove that when we know so little about him,[1] and in any case, how do we prove the general proposition that all the beliefs and claims of supremely good and sane people are true?[2] Others appeal to the religion that has grown out of the belief in Jesus' divinity, arguing in effect that Christian faith and experience as expressed in the New Testament and as still existing today is so manifestly the genuine article that the Christian doctrines they presuppose must be true.[3] But this argument is circular, for by what criteria do we judge the authenticity of Christian faith and experience, except Christian ones? Doctrine and piety are used within the religious system to test and support each other, in a way that holds for every other religion just as much as it does for Christianity. And in any case, the whole discussion in this paragraph is made unnecessary by the fact that nowadays even rather belligerently orthodox Christian scholars can freely declare that Jesus 'certainly did not proclaim himself Messiah,'[4] and that, 'On the basis of the evidence available we must conclude that Jesus did not teach that he was God, did not claim to be God, did not believe that he was God.'[5] All in all, we must conclude that at this time of day doctrinal questions cannot be settled by attributing dogmatic infallibility to sayings of Jesus culled from the Gospels. A rather more sophisticated procedure is called for.

The first step must be to analyse, to unravel and to find out where the shoe pinches. Our difficulties with the doctrine of the atonement arise at several levels, but the obvious starting-point is that as usually stated it depends upon a number of ideas which no longer have any application in modern culture. I mean in particular the ideas of sacrifice, sin, the incorporation of one person in another, and the transferability of both blame and merit from one person to another.

Sacrifice is one of the most ancient and universal of all religious institutions. It depends upon the idea that the way society works is a model for the way the whole natural order works. Society is governed by chiefs and kings. When approaching such figures, whether to pay homage, to present a petition or to seek one's own restoration to favour, it is fitting to offer a gift. Gifts strengthen bonds. Gifts are offered up, and favour flows down. Now if the cosmos is organized in the same sort of way that society is organized – and, after all, society is the single most powerful available model of a complex interdependent system – then it is fitting that we should behave towards the powers that control the cosmos in the same sort of way as we behave towards the human rulers of society. So whenever we approach the gods we should bring with us a gift. Since such gifts express our sincere devotion and our desire for favour, the most acceptable gift of all must be the complete and disinterested self-sacrifice to God of the most perfect man, made on behalf of the whole race.

Until early modern times the practice of sacrificing was so obviously appropriate and intelligible that it was scarcely necessary to theorize about it. But today the old style of personal monarchical control has largely vanished both from the cosmos and from human society. So far as we can recognize order in the cosmos at all, it is not an order of personal control from above but an impersonal, immanent and universal regularity of behaviour which is not going to be affected in any way by the practice of sacrifice. In society there has been a rather similar change; so far as society is orderly, it is ordered by general rules laid down by our duly-elected assemblies and duly-appointed officials. With this change there has come a change in morality which has eradicated the old social basis for sacrifice, for where once men spoke approvingly of gifts and favours they now speak disapprovingly of bribery and patronage.

This has meant that in modern society sacrifice has vanished so completely that learned men are obliged to invent theories to explain how it could once have been thought efficacious.[6]

The concept of sin has fared little better. It was originally based on the belief that God or the gods had laid down a ritual order within which human life must be lived. A system of sacred commands and prohibitions defined a number of boundaries which must not be crossed.[7] So long as you stayed within the boundaries you remained ritually pure and clean and you and all your people with you would receive many blessings; but if you 'transgressed' by crossing a boundary you became a sinner, one who was ritually impure or unclean. This state of uncleanness was highly contagious, and threatened to bring down supernatural sanctions not only upon your own head but on all society unless it was speedily rectified.

The crucial point is that the concept of sin was at first entirely ritual and not at all moral in the modern sense. As Nietzsche puts it, 'every deed is to be considered *solely with respect to its supernatural consequences*'.[8] In many societies you could hurt your neighbour a good deal, and such conduct did not attract the attention of the supernatural powers – provided, that is, that you had not violated a ritual boundary. If it happened that you both injured your neighbour and by the same act broke a sacred rule of respect, then the ritual transgression rather than the offence against a fellow man was the important fact in the case. Strictly speaking, sin was sin because it offended God and not because it hurt one's neighbour, and it was God rather than the neighbour who must be propitiated. You could sin unwittingly, and the consequences might be as dire as if the sin had been deliberate. You could incur defilement entirely innocently, as when a man fell sick because his wife had committed adultery without his knowledge. Such a person bore the supernatural punishment for another's sin, and nobody thought to complain that it is immoral that the world should work in such a way. Furthermore, since the surface of the human body was itself one of the most religiously-important frontiers, major ritual impurity could arise in areas which for us have no ethical content at all, such as the eating of unclean food or menstruation. And it is most important to note that ritual purity and impurity, being so contagious, created effects that rippled right through society, and were matters in which one person could act on behalf of others.

From early times the concept of sin began to be moralized. Gradually the requirement of God and the human claim of one's neighbour began to flow together and to coincide; gradually the defiling and the morally wrong have tended to become one and the same. Christianity has on the whole not wished to see religion simply identified with morality, for it rightly suspects that the complete moralization of sin is in effect the end of the concept of sin. So the process has been slow and hesitant, and even yet is not complete so far as many people are concerned. Throughout the Christian era there has been an odd mixture of the ritual and the ethical in the concept of sin, and almost up to modern times there has been a strong desire to distinguish sharply between doing something at God's command for God's sake and doing something for a merely human moral reason:

> I give no alms to satisfy the hunger of my brother, but to fulfil and accomplish the will and command of my God; I draw not my purse for his sake that demands it, but for his that enjoined it; I relieve no man upon the rhetorick of his miseries, nor to content mine own commiserating disposition; for this is still but moral charity and an act that oweth more to passion than reason.[9]

Those words are by a seventeenth-century writer. Nobody would write in such terms today, for to us it seems obvious that there is something cold and disagreeable about the piety that makes so sharp a distinction between God's command and human need as claims upon us. Evidently our religious thinking has become a good deal more humanitarian than it was even three centuries ago.

One result of the moralization of sin is well known: it has become difficult to accept that we are all born in a condition so defiled as to deserve God's just condemnation, and theologians have therefore set about revising the doctrine of original sin.[10] But still more important is the fact that the doctrine of the atonement always leaned heavily on just those archaic ritual elements in the idea of sin which have now vanished. That sin is primarily an offence against God rather than against one's neighbour; that it is socially highly contagious; that an innocent person may be defiled by and suffer supernatural punishment for the sins of other people;[11] that one person may approach God on behalf of many and procure for them the forgiveness of their sins; and that a supremely holy person's condition of purity and blessedness can be transmitted to others by some form of contact with him – all such ideas are ritual rather than ethical. The thoroughgoing moralization of the concept of sin, which began as far back as the pre-exile Israelite prophets and is today almost complete, has had the side-effect of making most traditional doctrines of the atonement seem immoral or unintelligible.

Many writers have said that it is a matter for congratulation that the church never formally committed itself to any one theory of the atonement, but has instead confined itself to reiterating the rich and varied New Testament imagery. Yes, indeed; for the best-known theories that have been put forward[12] are so highly mythological as to bewilder the modern student. They postulate that our eternal destiny has been determined for us by a strange transaction that has taken place in the supernatural world. In one account Christ outmanoeuvres the Devil and by a trick compels him to release his captive human souls; in another account Christ actually obtains a military victory over the Devil; in a third Christ's holy and blameless life is offered up to settle the immense accumulated debt of feudal service which the entire human race owes to God; in a fourth Christ is both priest and victim in offering himself up as a perfect sacrifice on behalf of us all; and in a fifth Christ endures in his own person and entirely innocently the punishment that we deserve, for the logic of morality requires that we should suffer but by the logic of ritual Christ suffers for us, and the ritual idea overrides the moral one to secure our redemption.

All such ideas are dead now. For a time interest shifted to the so-called 'exemplarist' or 'subjective' theories, which accord better with modern conceptions of moral freedom and individual responsibility. Jesus was seen as offering to us an inspiring example that affects our wills by kindling our imaginations. His voluntary death was an example of self-sacrificing love, or may be seen as an acted parable of the divine love. One strange and psychologically highly-disturbing theory sees in Jesus' death the climax of a self-mortifying grief and sorrow over human sinfulness.[13] But all such theories depend on our confidence that we have a vivid and clear picture of the historical Jesus. It is assumed that we can confidently say what kind of person he was and what his motives were; and such confidence can no longer be justified.

All received theories of Christ's work have broken down, both
the 'objective' theories that depend on now-lost ritual ideas and
the 'subjective' theories that depend on a vivid image of the
historical Jesus. We have no recourse left to us but to return to the
sources and begin again.

What we find gives us pause for thought. The long history of
Latin and Reformation theology has left us with ways of religious
thinking that use juridical metaphors to deal with problems in
psychology. The question posed is, 'Who is going to pay my debts
for me so that the Court can set me free? How can I be relieved of
the crushing burden of my sinfulness?' Even God was thought of
in these terms. He was imagined as caught in a dilemma, being
required by his justice to condemn me and by his mercy to acquit
me. A theory of the atonement was a theory of how God could
find a way to meet both demands and so extricate himself
honourably from the dilemma; and here again there was the same
curious mixture of legalism and psychologism.

On the evidence available, Jesus does not seem to think in these
ways. He does not postulate any special barrier that makes it
impossible either for God to forgive or for us to repent adequately.
On the contrary, he assumes that God's mercy is free-flowing and
that it lies within our power to choose a wholly new life.
Furthermore, the New Testament suggests that it is wrong to
think of Jesus as dying primarily to pay the price of my sins. The
circle of ideas involved was in fact much wider. It was believed
that God was bringing in an entirely new order of things, a world
of perfect bliss and fulfilment in which evil would be no more.
Jesus heralds this new age, is caught up in its birth-pangs, and
becomes the first to enter upon it. His death focusses and symbolizes the transition to the new era, and the communal experience
of the forgiveness of sins is only one of the many blessings that it
brings.

Later, when the expectation of the Kingdom of God receded
further and further into the future, the idea of redemption
narrowed and the believer began to ask himself, 'How can I, who
must now live indefinitely in this present evil world, obtain for
myself a supernatural guarantee of the forgiveness of my sins?'
Albert Schweitzer comments that, 'There is something cold and
unnatural about the naive egoism of such piety,'[14] but there is a
still more important point: because final redemption was so

remote, and because the believer took so pessimistic a view of this life, he was willing to pay almost any price for a guarantee of forgiveness strong enough to last to eternity. He positively demanded the development of authoritarian dogma and an objectified salvation-machine. Anything, so long as he could only obtain that guarantee; but as time went on the believer's insatiable anxiety and the oppressive institutions that it created took the faith further and further from Jesus. There is a true insight in Nietzsche's remark that 'Jesus had done away with the very concept "guilt" itself – he had denied any chasm between God and man, he *lived* this unity of God and man as *his* "glad tidings",' [15] for in an important sense Jesus did indeed operate at a level that made the very concept of sin irrelevant. There is a good deal of evidence that he declared the traditional ways of distinguishing between the clean and the unclean obsolescent and thereby overcame something characteristic of social religion in all ages, the close correlation between one's religious state and one's relation to the social order.

By social religion I mean this: Why is it that the righteous are always the pillars of the community and the sinners are always social outcasts? Evidently the righteous have inwardly identified themselves with the authority-principle in society. This has given them their strong sense of reality and their invincible assurance of their own entitlement to bind and to loose, to lay down the rules, and to define the terms on which the unfortunate sinners can be granted social rehabilitation. In social religion – legal establishment is neither here nor there – all religious concepts are in effect given a social meaning, so that religion is strictly bound to what Christianity once called 'the world'. God is the principle of social authority, a state of grace is a state of inward identification with that authority, sin is rebellion against it, and therefore makes one a social leper, conversion is the resolution of the Oedipus complex by internalizing and so submitting to social authority, forgiveness is social acceptance and righteousness is good social standing.

This entire complex of ideas which I have called 'social religion' appears to have been rejected by Jesus. It was precisely this which was under judgment and was passing away: salvation was final deliverance from it. A saying such as the one declaring that the publicans and the harlots go into the kingdom of God before the chief priests and the elders of the people[16] points to a really radical

transvaluation of all values. The particular way in which religion
has ordered society and given us our sense of reality that I have
called social religion has been so universal that we could not even
have become aware of it unless Jesus had pronounced judgment
upon it. Its destruction really does open up a new era.

Yet Christians say that the Kingdom of God has not come,
which is a mythological way of saying that the new order
proclaimed by Jesus has never been successfully institutionalized
in Christianity. In the early church, in the sects, in the Reformed
churches and in the Free churches the story is always the same –
after every attempt to overcome it, social religion has always
returned and re-established itself. But Jesus appears to have
proclaimed something different, a world in which we will be
delivered from the consciousness and even the very concept of sin.
Why? – Because the consciousness of sin is simply the inner
counterpart and the creation of the oppressive and alienating
system which I have called social religion. When social religion
comes to an end the religious psychology that belongs with it also
passes away. Sin loses its power; it dies because the socio-religious
system that created and used the consciousness of sin as a tool of
power is dead. Just as the true exorcism of evil spirits is the
disappearance of 'evil spirits' because the religious psychology
that needed them has been overcome, so the true forgiveness of
sins is the disappearance of 'sin' because the socio-religious world
that needed and exploited 'sin' has passed away.

But 'sin' is such a tempting tool of power that, as the immediacy
of the Kingdom of God faded and the faithful increasingly
demanded solid guarantees to sustain them, it came creeping
back, bringing with it all the concepts and the institutions of social
religion. Here is the meaning of Nietzsche's characterization of
Christianity as a religion of *ressentiment*.[17] When I no longer
experience the blessings of the new era as arising spontaneously
within my own heart I seek a substitute, and find it in the reflexive
conviction of my own righteousness that I can derive from casting
out heretics, apostates, infidels and every other sort of sinner.
Philadelphia comes to be built on a solid foundation of xenopho-
bia. People sometimes express surprise that a religion of love
turned into a system that was oppressive, intolerant, prejudiced
and persecuting. Did they not feel compunction? No, because
persecution was more than a religious duty, it had become a

religious necessity. The orthodox and righteous derived their assurance of salvation from it.

Replying to the objection that the great dogmatic definitions were presumptuous attempts to define the indefinable, apologists have often replied that it rests on a misunderstanding. Definition was almost always undertaken in response to the threat of heresy, 'to avert error rather than to define truth'.[18] Well, yes; but this defence is unintentionally revealing. The reverent agnosticism of the old Negative Way, when institutionalized, could easily turn itself into obscurantism and worse. Has the church in every century only been able to sustain its consciousness of its own faith by continually throwing people out, by a long series of acts of rejection and exclusion?

Ressentiment, the psychology of social religion, is still a problem today, as is shown by the alarming body of evidence accumulated by social psychologists during the past forty years.[19] Allport and Kramer, in 1946, found a high correlation between religious affiliation and anti-black prejudice, while in 1950 T. W. Adorno and others first described 'the authoritarian personality' and so stimulated a great deal of research. By today, as G. E. W. Scobie, himself a Christian minister, reports 'the correlation between religious conservatism and authoritarianism, prejudice, ethno-centrism and dogmatism seems to be well-established'.[20] It is true that social psychology is an infant science that lacks powerful general theories, and that most of the published material relates only to modern Europe and North America. Nevertheless, the discoveries are very disturbing, and it is particularly ironical that those who hold the most conservative doctrines in the most literal way, and make the strongest claims for their own converted lives, should come off the worst. Indeed, their doctrines are clearly falsified by their actual performance. The evidence is overwhelming that, for example, Catholics markedly over-achieve in criminality and under-achieve in science;[21] and that the American churches both black and white have so functioned as to maintain the inferior position of blacks in American society.[22] The religious score well in some respects, for they have happier marriages, better physical health and better personal adjustment in old age; but on the other hand religion seems to have little effect on moral behaviour and an adverse effect on moral attitudes.[23] The religious, and especially religious conservatives, appear to be of lower intelligence and creativity, more suggestible and less autonomous, more racist and less tolerant of social deviancy.[24] In America in the 1960s the Catholics were the most pro-war group, and the majority of anti-war demonstrators were persons of no religious affiliation.[25] A further example of the way the facts can reverse standard doctrinal stereotypes appears in the attitudes towards each other of different religious groups in an American city: the Protestants handed out the most adverse criticism and received the least, whereas the Jews were both the most tolerant and the most criticized group.[26]

It is not surprising that theologians and churchmen have been slow to discuss in public the problems created by these discoveries, though there have been one or two notable exceptions. Bishop James Pike in the United States was one such, and in Britain some Catholics have been willing to enquire into the connection between Catholic rates of violent crime and authoritarianism in church and family structures. Some Christian psychiatrists have been willing to draw attention to the disturbing effects in later life of a strict religious upbringing. In addition the relative liberalism of the clergy and changes in church teaching have measurably reduced prejudice in various areas during the last generation or so. Catholic antisemitism, for example, has now largely gone.[27]

More encouragingly, social psychologists, following a lead given by G. W. Allport in 1966, have found reasons for making a distinction between extrinsic and intrinsic religion.[28] The main empirical basis for the distinction is that the most devout are measurably less prejudiced, dogmatic and authoritarian than the main body of conventional and conservative believers. Extrinsic religion, found among Evangelicals and others who hold 'conservative' (i.e. literalistic and objectified) religious views, is religion used as a way of defending the personality and gaining high self-esteem and other benefits of membership in the religious group. But there is also intrinsic religion, to be found among the most devout, among active religious liberals and radicals and, very strikingly, among unbelievers and Jews. It may seem odd that the most religious and the unbelievers should approximate to each other, but the reason appears to be that these people's working 'faith' is less defensive and more inspirational because it has become more internalized and autonomous. They are people whose faith is liberating and gives meaning to their lives, and they are relatively tolerant and free from prejudice. They simply do not have the same psychological need for prejudice as do the more conventional and conservative believers. Their faith sufficiently confirms its own efficacy within their own lives, and they do not need to seek external reinforcement for it by making other people inferior.

This may be so, but Argyle and Beit-Hallahmi are not yet convinced. They allow that there is empirical evidence for the old idea that true believers do exist but are always a minority, and to that extent they allow that the concept of intrinsic religion does have application. But, say they, the question remains: 'Why is it that those who have no religious affiliation have consistently been found to be less prejudiced, more open-minded, and more tolerant towards minority groups? It seems that the positive correlation between irreligiosity and tolerance should be explained as well.' [29]

I think it can be explained. Experience of any major culture other than our own makes it reflexively clear to us that the irreligious in our own culture are not simply unbelievers, but Jewish or Christian unbelievers. Their humanism is still perceptibly a Jewish or Christian humanism, and it was reached historically by developing certain themes in the Bible. Beatrice Webb gives a typical case-history in her autobiography, *My Apprenticeship*. In youth her religious quest ranged widely before she was able to accept the implications of the fact that 'it was during middle decades of the nineteenth century that, in England, the impulse of self-subordinating service was transferred, consciously and overtly, from God to man'.[30] Yet she remained quite clearly a *Christian* agnostic and humanist, who maintained the practice of prayer all her life. She had found that so far as practical living is concerned the meaning of the two great commandments, to love God and to love one's neighbour, is summed up in the second; but in reaching this conclusion she was not abandoning Christianity. You could equally well say that her humanism and socialism represented a modern fulfilment of the Christian ideal of the active life. Social religion, with its in-group/out-group psychology and its use of dogma to distinguish the two groups from each other, naturally leads us to put all the religious Christian insiders in one camp and all the irreligious unbelievers in the other; and then it meets the difficulty that the most religious are more like the unbelievers than they are like their conservative and conventional fellow-Christians. Its inability to explain this anomaly makes it puzzled and resentful, as we see from popular attacks on liberal and radical Christians. But if we join Jesus and reject the categories of social religion, then the anomaly disappears. The real distinction, which explains the facts discovered by social psychology, is the distinction between the extrinsic religion of those who think in the categories of what I have called social religion, and the intrinsic religion of the most devout Christians, the Jews and the 'unbelievers'.

Now we can proceed: intrinsic Christian faith does exist, albeit only among a few. I take it that a Christian life is a life that is in every part shaped by the principle, 'Thou shalt love thy neighbour as thyself.' A fuller account of what this involves must be deferred; suffice it for the moment to refer to Kierkegaard's classic exposition.[31] I take it that there are people who do live such a life, and therefore that it is possible to resolve to live such a life and to succeed in doing so. But anyone who wishes to embark on such a life must clearly change a good deal, for his personality and his policies must be transformed. The difficulties involved are so great that it is reasonable for us to welcome anything that will help us to make the change, and to use any discipline of self-knowledge and self-examination that promises to help us test our progress. Such aids might include membership in a group of others who are following the same path, and exemplary stories which have the power to kindle the imagination. Above all rituals are useful – using the word ritual from now on to signify, not a sacred prohibition that forbids one to violate a frontier, but a socially approved ceremony that actually helps people to cross the frontier between one state or way of life and another. In every society such transitions are marked by rituals, and it seems to be a fact that these ceremonies do help to establish people in their new way of life. For instance, people who marry with religious rites form measurably more lasting marriages than people who do not, and people who have been able to bury their dead with all due ceremony are able to complete their mourning and make a new life more easily than people who have not been so fortunate. In these rituals certain great symbols are invoked, for they have been found to have the psychological power to carry the participant through the transition from the old state to the new one.

With these materials, which are all as I would claim matters of fact, I can define what I mean by confessing Christ as my Saviour. I mean simply that the symbol of the dying and rising Christ, enacted first in baptism and subsequently re-enacted in other rituals and in other ways, represents to me and continually helps me in the transformation of my personality and way of life to which I am pledged as a Christian.

This account is strictly rational and does not involve any supernaturalist metaphysics or mythology at all. With many of the classical theologians, it regards sacraments as efficacious signs, the criterion of their efficacy being simply ethical. The traditional doctrine that by his death and resurrection Christ has obtained for us the forgiveness of sins and opened the gates of heaven is to be understood in terms of the psychological and moral power of the Christian symbolism of death and rebirth; which after all is arguably what Paul and other New Testament writers are saying. There is to be no separating of Christ's resurrection from the risen life which believers should be living, for the former is simply an efficacious symbol of the latter.

Christ is here seen as symbolizing the principle of death and rebirth in the spiritual life. We are not able to envisage him as being an invisible person distinct from us and over against us, for although talk of invisible personal companions is still heard, it strains language so severely that we are bound to conclude that it has no clear meaning. In any case, moral faith is purer and more sincere without it.

Although there is no metaphysical link between Christ the symbol and the historical Jesus, there does remain an important historical connection. As we have seen, Jesus was an ironist and a prophet of religious awakening who sought to open men's eyes to a new order of things. The prospect of losing everything that seemed to give their lives meaning antagonized his hearers. It was to them the end of the world, for they were losing social religion and the reality that it constructs, the only world that most of them had ever known. This, with its implied demand that faith must become fully intrinsic and autonomous, was a kind of nihilism. The animosity Jesus provoked and endured bears indirect witness to the greatness of his message, and it led him to his martyrdom. That is the first sense in which he died for us.

Secondly, by his diagnosis and judgment of social religion — some people prefer phrases like 'the established religion of his day' or 'pharisaism', but I stick with my term for it — Jesus moved altogether beyond the region inhabited by the ideas of law, sin, guilt and the like. To overcome social religion was to pass beyond the alienated religious psychology that it creates. He promises deliverance from the consciousness of sin and the self-mutilating psychology of 'ever-deepening penitence'. Here is a second sense in which he is the Saviour, which does much to justify the traditional belief that before him all religion was extrinsic.

Thirdly, he is the Saviour in the sense that his death and resurrection have from the beginning been found to be efficacious symbols of the new way of life he inaugurated.

However, it must be acknowledged in conclusion that our account of Christ's saving work is, strictly speaking, logically independent of the truth of any historical statements about Jesus. If the Christian way of life is intrinsically worth living just for its own sake, and if the symbols, rituals and other aids do in fact help us to live it, then that is in principle sufficient. Other symbols and rituals may also be efficacious, and the historical connection is only contingent. Nevertheless, we have drawn on ideas that can be traced back to the beginnings of Christianity, and perhaps even to Jesus himself, and have found great profit in doing so. Thus although the historical connection is contingent, we have found that it is valuable and should be cherished.

7

CHRIST (IV): THE NEW HUMANITY

The supernatural Christ of faith who is set forth in the church's hymns, doctrines and festivals is a strange and awesome figure. In the great tradition of Byzantine and Eastern Orthodox painting they achieved a representation of him comparable in its grandeur with the Buddha-image in Asian sculpture. Piety confesses him and theology articulates doctrine about him; but what kind of being is he? What is his precise status?

This question scarcely arose before modern times. In the old days, talk of gods and other supernatural persons was embedded in a cultural context in which it seemed obviously intelligible. People reckoned they knew what they were talking about. Today that is no longer so, mainly because mechanistic explanation of events not directly caused by human beings has proved to be so much more powerful than the older style of explanation in terms of hidden purposes; while in the case of the supernatural Christ there is the additional difficulty that in modern times he has become partly disconnected from the historical Jesus. The upshot is that much of what is said about Christ is now very perplexing, and it is infuriating to read dozens of volumes of christology and never once be told just how and at what level the authors intend us to take their statements. Today, the philosophy-of-religion question comes first: until it is answered, we don't know what we are talking about. What kind of being *is* the Christ of faith?

The true answer can be glimpsed if we begin by using a distancing device, directing the question in the first place to Christ's feminine counterpart, the Blessed Virgin Mary. Her historical origins are even more obscure than his, for the critical historian can scarcely claim for her more than her name, her home village, her relation to Jesus, and a probability that she joined with other members of his family in disapproving of his activities.[1] Yet she also slowly developed into a great supernatural figure around whom there gathered a cycle of doctrines, festivals and devotional practices closely modelled on his. In the case of Jesus the historical basis for doctrines like those of his virginal conception and bodily ascension to heaven is decidedly tenuous: in the case of the corresponding doctrines about Mary it is non-existent. Nevertheless, piety has uninhibitedly created a Mary of faith who has far outsoared the shadowy Mary of history. In short, Mary, although she is both more modest in her origins and lower in her final rank in the system, appears to be a more extreme case of the same kind as Jesus; so what sort of object can the Mary of faith be?

Sophisticated mariologists tell us – orally, if not in cold print – that Mary functions as an ideal symbol of the church in general and of each human soul in particular in its response to God's grace. Her glory does not set her over all other Christians, but rather represents what is promised to them. Venerating her, believers commit themselves to the values she personifies – love, purity, obedience, receptivity to grace and the ideals of Catholic family life. Because she is thought of as a person, she has many facets and can present herself in slightly different manners as an ideal for priests, for nuns, for mothers, for young girls and so on. Through their devotion to her, various classes of believer can each express in their different ways their desire to become what they see her to be. The prayers officially prescribed for her feasts confirm this interpretation, for in them believers repeatedly ask that by following her example they may come to share her qualities.

Someone who explains and defends mariology in these terms admits to functioning at two different levels. As a believer he thinks of and addresses Mary in realistic language that suggests that she is a real person out there, but at the critical, commenting, philosophical level of thinking he knows that there is not 'really' a Mary out there. Rather, Mary is a personified religious ideal. Clearly I can have no quarrel with this, for in our time we cannot help functioning in such a two-levelled way, and indeed I interpret the whole of Christian supernatural doctrine along these lines.

We speak realistically in our prayers, but we must do so in the knowledge that 'really' such language is mythological – that is, symbolic, expressive and action-guiding. Also, I set aside the question of whether all the qualities of character that are associated with Mary are really as desirable as they are claimed to be. That question, highly important in other contexts, is not relevant here. What is relevant is that Mary's case suggests that when we venerate a supernatural person what we are really doing is setting up a personified ideal that we aspire after and to which we pledge ourselves.

Since historically Mary has been so closely modelled on Christ, it is reasonable to guess that what is true in her case may also be true in his. Piety addresses Christ in realistic language as if he were an invisible divine person out there, but perhaps at the philosophy-of-religion level we shall have to recognize that he functions as an ideal symbol of what mankind as a whole and each human person is to become. He is the 'Last Man', or the 'Second Adam'.

This suggestion is confirmed by the fact that in both cases the burgeoning complexity of the language used seems to rule out a realistic interpretation of its meaning. Mary stands for the church as a whole, shows slightly different faces at each of her major sanctuaries, asks somewhat different virtues of different classes of her devotees, and although strictly-speaking she is only a finite human person, she functions so competently as a kind of private secretary to God that she is able to deal with petitions and obtain boons on behalf of millions of humble individuals simultaneously. Christ also is both universal and highly particular, for he is both the future totality of redeemed and perfected humanity and a person who dwells in the heart of each individual believer. His one sacred body walked in Palestine, is the church, dwells in heaven and rests on altars. The idioms that are used are so wide-ranging and complex, that although they may be grammatically of a descriptive kind, it is, I suggest, obvious on reflection that they cannot 'literally' be descriptive. The language must be seen as a symbolic vehicle for expressing religious feeling, aspiration, commitment and hope. It has the fluid, evocative character of poetry and myth rather than the more tightly-controlled logic of descriptive, fact-stating language.

This suggests that the exalted Christ is indeed a personified symbol of the Christian hope for humanity. The ancient belief in his return to earth in glory is an expression of the hope that the new human possibilities which Jesus has opened up will one day be fully actualized here on this earth. What he is, all men will be. The exalted Lord was at first a very strongly eschatological figure. Devotion to him was a way of expressing the communal faith that through what Jesus had set in motion there would one day come a renewal of humanity and of all the world.

If in order to develop this interpretation we turn now to the sources, we have to acknowledge at the outset that the origins of Christianity as a distinct faith focussed around the person of the exalted Jesus are very obscure. Had a cult of Jesus' own person begun during his lifetime we would expect there to be a good deal more evidence of it in the Synoptic Gospels than in fact there is. What little we do find appears to be the product of post-Easter revision of some of his sayings.

When did the cult of Jesus begin? The Acts of the Apostles may preserve evidence of a very primitive doctrine held in the earliest Jerusalem church, to the effect that Jesus had been the final prophet expected by the Jews. He had announced the imminent arrival of God's reign and had called for national repentance, but had been rejected like the prophets before him and had suffered martyrdom. Now God had rewarded this faithful service by designating him the Messiah-to-be. Soon the Kingdom would be inaugurated with the returned Jesus as its King.[2]

If this was indeed the earliest form of the Christian faith, it need not have required the risen Jesus to be either a very active figure or even as yet the object of personal devotion. He may well have been thought of as hidden and dormant until the great day of his vindication, when God would as it were re-activate him and restore him in glory to earth.

However, the focussing of faith around Jesus' person did undoubtedly begin very early. The strongest evidence we have for the earliest Christian tradition lies in those passages where Paul mentions the traditions that he was himself taught, or that he thinks he can safely assume his readers to have been taught. Of these passages, the best known describes the institution of the Eucharist.[3] It shows that even as early as the 40s, the community at Jerusalem already held that Jesus had spoken the words 'This is my body' and 'This cup is the new covenant in my blood' at the last supper with his disciples. Now these words cannot in fact go back to Jesus himself, for they presuppose a great deal of theology that could only have been worked out in response to Jesus' death.[4] They assume that Jesus' death has occurred and has come to be seen as a sacrifice inaugurating a new covenant, that Jesus has already entered into the promised new era, and that through ritual re-enactment of the last supper believers can participate in his covenant-sacrifice and so come to share with him in the blessings of the new age. None of this would have been intelligible during Jesus' lifetime, when the disciples had no way of knowing what was to be the manner and the meaning of his death. But at any rate the Jerusalem church had worked it all out by the 40s, and it does give a clue to the process by which the developing faith became focussed upon Jesus' person. The church held that the new era proclaimed by Jesus could be glimpsed in him, and had even been entered upon by him through his death. In the Eucharist, as in baptism, ritual solidarity with Jesus in his death was a means by which believers could enjoy a foretaste of the coming age and could be assured that when he came as king they would be ready to live and reign with him. 'As often as you eat this bread and drink the cup, you proclaim the Lord's death until he comes,' said the apostle, and 'Maranatha!' (Our Lord, come!) replied the faithful.

From this starting-point the idea of solidarity with Jesus reached back and reshaped many of his remembered sayings. Believers were to follow him, to take up the cross, to be baptized with a baptism like his, to remember that when even two or three of them met together he was present, and in time of persecution to be sustained by the thought that he stood with them as they stood with him.

However (to put it in our terms rather than theirs), this solidarity with Jesus was a matter of ritual, of morality and of hope rather than a metaphysical bond between the world below and the world above. The exalted Lord was one who is to come rather than one who is above, an ideal object rather than a metaphysical one. The point is vital, for the revelatory force of the message of the earthly Jesus had depended upon his evocation of an absolute disjunction between two worlds and two value-scales, the world that is and the world that is to come, the relative and the absolute standards for appraising human life. There could be no final redemption and no deliverance from social religion unless that disjunction was maintained. The two worlds could not have been thought of as co-existing, one below and one above, for so to think of them is in effect to say that Christ's new world is nothing but the metaphysical foundation of this present world. That is the deep and terrible mistake made by the mainstream of realist theology: it equated the distinction between this world and the Kingdom of God with the philosopher's distinction between appearance and reality, and so reduced the objects of religious aspiration to the status of being no more than the hidden reality of the way things are now. But no: until this world has wholly passed away, until the believer has passed through annihilation, the new world cannot come. There must be a radical break. So, while the old world remains, the exalted Christ must be seen as an ideal symbol of hope, as one who is yet to be and not as one who metaphysically already is.

At first this insight was maintained, for the belief in Jesus' exaltation did not subvert, but rather heightened, the sense of contrast between the two orders. The exalted Jesus was only just off stage, hidden in the wings, and might at any moment burst upon the scene. But with the passage of time the faith became steadily less eschatological and more realist-metaphysical. As the church became less concerned with proclaiming a new order and more concerned with its establishment in the present order, so Jesus' exaltation in heaven increasingly became not a brief and tense interlude but an end in itself, a permanent metaphysical fact which replaced the original hope. Jesus was being converted from an ideal object of eschatological expectation into a Being in the world above, and the longer he remained in heaven the less he threatened the *status quo* on earth and the more he ratified it. As Christ Almighty the cosmic Lord, he began to be seen as a stabilizing and validating principle, until he ended by endorsing and hallowing all the things that the earthly Jesus had prophesied against. For the original Jesus, salvation lay on the far side of the utter dissolution of the world, but Christendom increasingly reinstated the ancient pagan principle that salvation lies in bringing all aspects of earthly life here below into harmony and conformity with the heavenly and eternal cosmic order. The social and ecclesiastical realm here below was seen as mirroring eternal realities, and believers needed only to undergo an entirely painless symbolic death and rebirth in infant baptism and thereafter to live piously and obediently within the established sacred this-worldly scheme of things to be sure of salvation. It was the ancient easy way to salvation through cosmic harmony, and not the new way of dissolution and recreation.

However, after the rise of classical physics from Galileo to Newton had broken down the old distinction between the earth and the heavens, the idea that earthly life ought to be conformed to standards of perfection laid up in the unchanging heavens was evidently doomed. Religious thought was increasingly compelled to turn from cosmology back to history. It looked again at its sources, and found there that the early Christians had looked not so much up for authority as forward in hope. How was this ancient eschatological faith to be reappropriated and restated in modern circumstances? By developing liberal theologies of progress, and radical theologies of hope, of the future and of human liberation. But, for reasons that no doubt have to do with the politics of religious truth, modern theology has been slow to admit openly that when your categories of religious thinking become historical rather than metaphysical you must cease to regard the exalted Christ as a metaphysical object and must instead see him as a symbol of human destiny and as an ideal object of aspiration. It has been even slower to see that the original dynamic of the Gospel *required* this latter interpretation. Worse still, the difficulty of reviving eschatological hope today was seriously underestimated, and theology in consequence has related itself to modern culture at much too shallow a level. It contracted too easy an alliance with various forms of secular belief in human progress and perfectibility. The belief in progress, whether held in its Enlightenment, its liberal, or its Marxist form, was merely a piece of ideology, a secular myth that expressed the confident expansionist mood of Western culture in the later eighteenth and nineteenth centuries. It postulated that by the operation of necessary laws of historical development, or by the evolution towards perfect self-consciousness of the world-spirit, a grand process of cosmic betterment was unfolding. By the end of the nineteenth century, for those who had eyes to see, this belief was already coming to an end, and Nietzsche had sent it up in flames. It was nothing but superstition, animism, another fiction that had had its day; and theology should have known better than to espouse it.

By now we have been deprived of all objective grounds for optimism about the long-term prospects for either the cosmos or the human race. Since the time of Giordano Bruno at the end of the sixteenth century it had become common to imagine that every star had a planetary system and every planet was inhabited.[5] The cosmos was thought to be teeming with life. But the further our actual investigations have extended, the more these fancies have been disappointed and the more unspeakably vast, alien and impersonal the cosmos in fact appears to be. Our knowledge is still very limited, but there is precious little evidence to support those otherwise hard-headed scientists who hope for contact with extra-terrestrial life-forms and speak of prolonging our collective human life-span by somehow overcoming the limits set by the velocity of light and colonizing other parts of the galaxy. So far as our best knowledge can yet tell us, we are transient products of a vast inexorable process that is destined to wipe us out as indifferently as it brought us into being, and that is that.

The ultimate fate of the cosmos remains uncertain because its total mass is still undetermined. It may expand for ever until the last star has decayed and only a silent sea of radiation is left, or it may begin to contract back again to the point from which it began. If so, it may or may not be oscillating. Although the question is one of great theoretical interest, it is of less practical moment than the fact that the cosmos at least appears to offer our race a very long, albeit finite, span of collective life before us, provided only that we can find some way of ordering our affairs rationally. However, the scene here on earth confounds that qualified optimism. Everywhere people's first allegiance is to their own nation, tribe, class, race or faith rather than to the species and to the Earth. The Earth's resources are finite, and competition for them is severe. Though resilient, the ecosphere is fragile and may break down. World production of many commodities peaked a decade ago and now slowly declines while world population continues to rise. Across entire continents people find they must live with little prospect of ever seeing the establishment of even a moderately free, just and prosperous political order, and hopes that either the Communist Party or the United Nations might be able to bring in a better order of things have been bitterly disappointed. Religion is more often a threat to peace than an instrument of it. Worst of all, we have already lived for about thirty years with the knowledge that the human race is entirely capable of largely destroying itself at a few hours notice. Attempts to negotiate general disarmament have failed, while the steady advance of technology progressively increases the risk of nuclear suicide. Nobody knows what the odds are, but everybody can sense that they are shortening.

It is because the scene around us offers so few objective grounds for optimism that liberal and *marxisant* theologies of the future so often have the air of ineffectual ranting. We have seen too much and have become too disillusioned for them to get any real purchase on our thinking. A theology of revolution may gather a small crowd of curious onlookers for a while, but soon a heckler will point out that on average Third World countries already enjoy revolutionary changes of government every six years or so, and what good does it do them? The more a government describes itself as revolutionary, the more tyrranical we can be sure it is. As for the longer-term human and cosmic prospect, even so robustly confident a liberal theologian as Hans Küng is obliged to confess that he can see no way of harmonizing the religious images with the scientific theories, and to content himself with moral resolutions and a very unspecific declaration of hope.[6]

The optimistic theologies of liberalism, of hope, of the future and of revolution are weak because they wedded themselves to the secular myth of progress at the very time when that secular faith was itself obsolescent. Like the metaphysical theologies of Christendom they never even reached the question of eschatology, but were content to interpret Christian concepts in terms of this world's needs and hopes. They failed to begin with a sufficiently deep and courageous analysis of the modern cultural crisis, probably because they were so strongly committed to the use of critical ways of thinking in religious questions that they refused to recognize that the critical spirit might itself be leading modern culture towards a catastrophe.

It had all begun harmlessly enough. Christianity had itself nurtured the sceptical, enquiring, testing, demythologizing, iconoclastic and critical spirit which in modern times first emerges into the light of day, fully conscious of itself and its powers, in René Descartes. This critical spirit brings to the search for truth a ruthless honesty, a tenacious ingenuity and a refusal to be deceived that must owe something historically to the scrupulous self-examination of Christian penitents. When it appeared as the driving force behind modern philosophy and science, it was widely assumed that it would be beneficial. It would act as a healthy purge, it would drive out superstition, it would be a powerful instrument for the discovery of new truth, and it might bring about a second Reformation. Few could see where it might eventually lead, and those few were not taken seriously by the rest. Theologians embraced it eagerly and hopefully, and we often find them ending by expressing a pained innocent astonishment at the conclusions to which it has led them. David Friedrich Strauss, for example, ended his great book by freely acknowledging the collision with traditional faith to which his 'critical and speculative views' had led him. But, he says in effect, don't blame me, for it just turned out that way:

> . . . this collision is not the effect of the curiosity of an individual; it is necessarily introduced by the progress of time and the development of Christian theology; it surprises and masters the individual, without his being able to guard himself from it.[7]

Tragic necessity was similarly invoked by Albert Schweitzer in his final comments on the quest for the historical Jesus. The all-out application of critical thinking to the problem of Christian origins was 'a uniquely great expression of sincerity, one of the most significant events in the whole mental and spiritual life of humanity', he declares; but by 'an inevitable necessity . . . the work which historical theology thought itself bound to carry out . . . fell to pieces just as it was nearing completion.'[8]

As Schweitzer saw it, the basic contradiction was that between the modern period's irrevocable commitment to world-affirmation and the radically world-negating Jesus who had been discovered by criticism. It was not that the quest had failed, but rather that it had been forced to the conclusion that the true and original Jesus had been so alien a figure as to be irrelevant to modern Christianity. The most that Schweitzer could claim on Jesus' behalf was that modern world-affirmation 'must in the individual spirit be Christianized and transformed by the personal rejection of the world which is preached in the sayings of Jesus'.[9] Jesus could not threaten modern world-affirmation, but he might still be used to purify it. Schweitzer at this stage in his career assumed that modern world-affirmation was secure – indeed, that it was a duty to help to keep it secure – and so the function of critical Christian faith was not to challenge it or to offer a radical alternative to it, but merely to purge and strengthen it. Even the great rediscoverer of eschatology himself could not see the relevance of it to the modern cultural crisis. He lived in an interim period when, although Christian supernatural doctrine was crumbling, it still seemed to many that the moral order, the concept of human nature, and so our sense of reality would hold firm. He did not recognize how completely the critical demythologizing spirit would dissolve away the moral order and even the world itself. Only after the Second World War did he write that 'we are today at the beginning of the end of the human race'[10] and see that after all these centuries the original Jesus is at last returning to contemporaneity with us. At the time when he wrote *The Quest of the Historical Jesus* he seems to have been unaware that the will to truth had reached thoroughgoing nihilism twenty years earlier.[11]

Yet both Schweitzer and Strauss had seen a certain necessity in the advance of criticism, as if it were a force that once unleashed is unstoppable. Why so? Why must it sweep everything before it so that, whatever the topic, in every conflict between conservative and critical views the critical one must eventually prevail, however long and hard-fought the battle? It is because the relationship between the two mentalities is asymmetrical. A critical position can understand a conservative one without itself ceasing to be critical, whereas a conservative or dogmatic position cannot come to understand a critical one without itself becoming critical. Once you understand the choice, you are on the critical side of the gulf. Traffic between the two points of view can move in one direction only. Because the conservative so closely relates truth to the needs and authority of the social order, it seems appropriate to him to use all sorts of political devices to protect tradition from infection by the spirit of criticism. The critic finds his arguments denounced, blocked, resisted, excluded and stigmatized. But however difficult it is made to cross over from a pre-critical to a critical mentality, once you have made the transition it is irreversible. The critical outlook advances extremely slowly but very surely, for it can only gain adherents and cannot lose them.

Many modern people, distressed by the thought that more and more is being dissolved away and taken from them, would like to think that we have a free choice in the matter. They talk as if one might set critical and traditional ways of thinking about some topic side by side, consider their relative merits, and decide which to adopt. But this is an illusion. You can't go home again, for the very ability to suspend belief and step outside one's own ways of thinking sufficiently to be able to appraise some fundamentally-different system of thought – the very idea that one *has a choice* and a *right to choose* in such matters – shows that one is already irreversibly committed to critical thinking. Only for critical thinking does the possibility of such a choice even arise. And we are already most of the way towards nihilism, for in supposing that we are free to contemplate and choose between different basic systems of thought, we are already presuming that such systems are but humanly-evolved constructions, shaped by the social and psychological needs they were evolved to meet, and to be appraised merely by the criterion of their success in meeting those needs. Thus John Stuart Mill, writing about the Victorian debate between believers and unbelievers, points out that those who argued that religion is a vitally important and beneficial influence in society, giving stability, meaning and happiness to human lives and so forth, had already conceded the main issue to the sceptic.[12] Their own selection of arguments and a ground to fight on ought itself to have been enough to warn the conservatives that things had already gone a great deal further than they realized.

There has been a strong tendency in modern English-language philosophy to shift from a correspondence to a pragmatist theory of truth, and so from an empiricist to a constructivist theory of knowledge. Pure empiricism has tended to break down, because it is so hard to see how our knowledge-systems can really be given objectivity by being tested against pure, objective, theory-neutral experience. How can we even specify what such experience *is*? Is it not the case that all our experience is shaped by theories? The notion of a pure datum of experience, like the notion of completely formless matter, seems to be a mirage which vanishes the harder one tries to pin it down. It is not solid and independent enough to do the checking job for which it is required. Well, pragmatism does not at first seem very alarming, and it seems easy enough to shift from a correspondence to a pragmatist view of religious truth and get into the way of talking about religious beliefs entirely in terms of our duty to hold them, the good they do and the moral policies they require of us. It seems easy enough, for there is considerable traditional warrant for talking in this way, and nearly everybody does so talk nowadays (though usually with the precaution of covering his tracks by making conservative noises); but to grasp the implications of this kind of move, to see why the advance of critical thinking has forced it upon us, and – above all – to be truthful about where it is leading us: that is another matter entirely.

So where does the critical spirit eventually lead? The history of modern philosophy since Hume gives some indication of the answer, although it was not until the end of the nineteenth century that it was clear how shrewd a prophet Hume had been. Philosophy has tended to demythologize not merely traditional religious belief but also everything else that has been proposed as a substitute for it in its function of anchoring human life. 'Scepticism regarding morality is what is decisive,' remarks Nietzsche, adding that the feeling that 'everything lacks meaning' arose because 'the untenability of one interpretation of the world, upon which a tremendous amount of energy has been lavished, awakens the suspicion that *all* interpretations of the world are false'.[13] Scepticism about an objective moral order built into the world was obviously implicit from the very beginnings of modern science, which from the time of Mersenne and Descartes had been successful just insofar as it remained on a mechanistic course; but it was only at the end of the nineteenth century that the natural sciences began to offer a reasonably complete and widely-understood cosmology and to become the foundation of modern culture. It was at about that time that the triumph of science in the culture coincided with the disintegration of the public moral order.

In a note written at Nice in the winter of 1887–8,[14] Nietzsche describes how the illusions of aim, unity and being are unmasked. The illusion of aim is the long, fruitless struggle to discover a 'meaning' in all events,

the fulfilment of some highest ethical canon, . . . the moral world-order, or the growth of love and harmony in the intercourse of beings; or the gradual approximation of a state of universal happiness; or even the development towards a state of universal annihilation (Nietzsche probably has Buddhism in mind, DC) – any goal at least constitutes some meaning. What all these notions have in common is that something is to be *achieved* through the process – and now one realizes that becoming aims at *nothing* and achieves *nothing*.

The second illusion, that of unity, arises when one has postulated 'a totality, a systematization, indeed any organization in all events, and a soul that longs to admire and revere has wallowed in the idea of some supreme form of domination and administration'. When a person contemplates the loss of this idea he discovers that 'at bottom, man has lost the faith in his own value when no infinitely-valuable whole works through him; i.e., he conceived such a whole in order to be able to believe in his own value' – and this realization of his own motives completes the demythologization of his thinking.

The third illusion is that of being. When we recognize that the world has no aim and no grand unity, we reject it as 'appearance' and take refuge in a 'real' world beyond it. The values which we failed to find in this world are seen as laid up in a true and eternal world which is our real home. But in time people come to recognize that 'that world is fabricated solely from psychological needs', and so again they are disappointed.

Thus the will to truth, on Nietzsche's account, leads us to regard as fictitious all the ideas with which we have tried to give the world value and so draw from it ethical guidelines for ourselves. They are no more than 'perspectives of utility, designed to maintain and increase human constructs of domination'.[15] And this point of view, by demythologizing not merely traditional religion but also such substitutes for it as idealist philosophy, Marxism, progress, psycho-analysis, an immaterial mind, the freedom of the will, objective *a priori* knowledge and even reason itself, leads to the crisis of meaninglessness as described, for example, in existentialist philosophy. The will to truth had become dissociated from the will to maintain the social order, and had become entrenched in permanent and growing communities of people devoted to the pursuit of truth for its own sake, as far back as the seventeenth century. Their activity was bound to have the long-term effect of unmasking all the beliefs which had traditionally sustained the social order – and, in due course, all proposed replacements for them. The will to truth is liable to keep us trapped in the nihilism to which it has led us, for it makes us ask of any doctrine *cui bono?*, who stands to gain by it? Thus even so seemingly soft and easy-going a doctrine as utilitarianism, with its rational bureaucrats, welfare economics and consumerism, can be diagnosed as a conspiracy to dominate us.[16]

During the present century, English-language philosophy has adopted a very consciously cool and professional manner, and it finds rhetoric embarrassing, but it is certainly aware both that moral philosophy is central to the whole task of philosophy, and that moral philosophy is in severe trouble – which is in effect to say, in cool language, much the same thing as the existentialists have said. Some of its typical doctrines, such as 'emotivism' and 'prescriptivism', have been cool equivalents of existentialist doctrines. In rhetorical language, we have experienced not merely the death of the old metaphysical guarantor-God, but also the breakdown of the moral order, the real world and man himself. 'The death of man' is the impossibility of fixing a publicly acknowledged standard conception of human nature in a modern fast-changing pluralistic society, in which there is no standard conception of the good for man and no agreed method of solving moral questions, and in which we each of us play several distinct rôles, behaving somewhat differently in each of them. It is a time of dissolution, in which all human knowledge-systems and frameworks of understanding have come to be seen as disputable and transient. Human life is no longer held in and undergirded by an enduring coherent moral framework. Once only a few philosophers knew this, but now everyone knows it: it is our eschatological crisis. Jesus' eschatology was linked with a moral protest against what was earlier called social religion, whereas ours is linked with its final intellectual breakdown. But the implications are as great for our time as for his, and it is in this area that the connection between the early Christian movement and modern culture has to be made.

Jesus asked, 'What will you choose to be and to do when everything passes away and you face the Void?' When social religion has become so finally discredited that no attempt to smuggle it back again in new and updated forms can remain undetected for long; when truth can no longer bear to be used as an instrument of control and domination; and when objective constraints have been so reduced that almost every question becomes a moral question, because it is for us to decide in what way our knowledge-systems shall develop and in what way society shall be remade – then, the ethic of the Kingdom of God begins to look like practical politics. When the foundations of the present order are seen to have collapsed, then what seemed previously to have been a remote and impossible dream comes close.

Here are the first steps: the old world crumbled because the will-to-truth progressively exposed every idea it had sought to live by as ideological, i.e., an instrument of domination. The human being was reduced to a series of disparate roles, all of which are exposed as power-relations; he is only able to get a sense of his own worth by thieving it from others, whom he then despises for the worthlessness to which he has reduced them. Such are the righteous and the unclean. And when power-knowledge and power-value are thus unmasked, the only spirituality that can stand is one based on complete disinterestedness.

Christian language has been so oppressively egoistic for so long that it is very hard for a Christian to learn disinterestedness, in spite of its ostensible prominence in the scheme of Christian values. Spinoza says, 'He who loves God must not expect to be loved in return.' Can we learn *that*? Goethe, commenting on Spinoza's saying, adds, 'If I love you, is that your concern?'[17] Can we learn *that*? Only after a good deal of unlearning: but it is only disinterested and fully altruistic neighbour love, expressed in truly just social institutions, that can restore human dignity. Value cannot be thieved. It has to be given, free.

The exalted Christ symbolizes that better state of humanity which one day we must choose. His 'glorious scars' symbolize what we must go through to reach it. His exaltation and sovereignty are not yet another form of domination over us, but symbolize a condition that we must aspire to. To worship him is to commit oneself to attempting to become a Christian, by attempting to bring into being the world he stands for.

8

PASSING THROUGH THE FIRE

A picture has been developing, and its main outlines are now visible. We have seen that the Christian movement began with a revolt against social religion inspired by the conviction that an entirely new order of things was not just possible, but very close. The prophets had had intimations of it, and now its hour had come.

The founder was a provincial radical teacher, a man sufficiently marginal to the established system to be able to see it from outside and sufficiently forceful, eloquent and original to become the point around which a new perception crystallized. The essential insight was, to put it in incongruously modern terms, that existing practice followed all too closely the pattern of Emile Durkheim's theory of religion.[1] It was sociological. It had fused the principle of religious authority with the principle of social authority, so that the religious value-scale was objectified socially. Social life was governed and shaped by an elaborate sacred Law, so that all religious meanings and states of the person were understood in terms of various concrete relations to the social order. In such a system the individual's religious standing before God was equated with his objective standing in society. The only way to gain the spiritual individuation and worth which every individual seeks as his life-project was the way of strict social conformity. He must become 'clean', one of the righteous. The actualization of religious value in human life depended upon, and was indeed identical with, the social duty to maintain in everyday practice clear distinctions between the clean and the unclean, the righteous and the sinners, the in-group and the out-group. There would not in fact *be* any rigteousness without that clear, socially-enforced line between the righteous and the sinners. The righteous needed the sinners, for they derived their own righteousness from them. The righteous were in the truth and had a strong sense of reality, for in such a system truth and reality are what the socio-religious authority-principle makes them, and there can be no alternative. There is no other truth or reality than that which the God of the righteous constitutes, and which their socio-religious system expresses. That is what was *meant* by saying that the God who is convenanted to our society and is its authority-principle is the Creator of the world, and can brook no rival.

To challenge such a system as oppressive and to see the righteousness it offered as bogus required profound originality, for one had to envisage the end of a world and of a particular form of religious existence. Tradition declares that it was John the Baptist whose eschatological preaching and baptism of repentance prepared the way. One day there came to John a disciple who received more than John knew he was giving, and in whom the old order was simply washed away. Religion as a heteronomous demand-system objectified in social structures became obsolete. It had never produced and never could produce anything like what had now appeared. It had merely sanctified the relation of oppressor to victim, on the basis of an authoritarian conception of God and of religious Law. Now a new reality was appearing that was especially welcomed by those whom the old system had defined as religiously worthless. They must renounce the old order and all its characteristic ways of thinking, they must undergo an inner transformation like that which Jesus had experienced in the Jordan river, and they must prepare for a new Kingdom of love, a covenant-brotherhood based on the principle of unconditional value-conferring altruism. Although for historical reasons the new society was spoken of as a kingdom, it would have nothing in common with traditional forms of kingship and authority.[2] The Kingdom of God could hardly be simply an objective theocracy, for an objective theocracy already existed and was precisely what was being rejected. In the new order God would no longer be regarded as an objective authority that generated and justified the clean/unclean distinction and the in-group/out-group psychology, but would be known only 'in secret'[3] as the principle of the disinterested neighbour-love that filled each believer. The social world would be all gift, so that the old system which authorized and instructed you to gain religious value for yourself by thieving it from somebody else would vanish. There could be no difference any more between receiving and giving, self-love and neighbour-love, being forgiven and bestowing forgiveness. The power-relations which had given to every human relationship the flavour of one between a debtor and a creditor were abolished. In the old system, religious value had been looked on with great anxiety as a scarce resource that must be fenced about to stop it from leaking away and being dissipated, and that must be kept pure by a most meticulous attention to rights, distinctions and regulations. But when it welled up inexhaustibly in everybody such anxiety would vanish. A new world, a new humanity was appearing.

The initial impulse did not last long. The fading of the early hope inevitably led to the concurrent reinstatement of social religion in a new, more generalized and Christianized form. Even within the gospel tradition Jesus is already to be found portrayed, incredibly, as giving his disciples the power to bind and to loose and as laying down a procedure for the excommunication of sinners from the church.[4] To this extent the Roman Catholic Cardinal was correct when he argued recently that 'the position of the Pope is implicit in Scripture itself'.[5] Indeed it is, for the leadership among Jesus' followers quickly took over the same sort of rôle in the church that the Pharisees and Sadducees had played in the Jewish nation, defining reality, saying who was in and who was out, fencing off the sacred and creating innumerable ritual distinctions. Back came the old debtor-creditor ways of thinking, especially in man's relation to God. Judaism had been social religion with prophetic hints of something better to come; Christianity became social religion with a hint that there had been something better at the beginning. But at least enough was remembered to nourish a radical tradition which could erupt from time to time in the future.

The essential feature of Christianized social religion, or Christendom, is that in it the will to truth and the will to affirm and defend the social order coincided as a single sacred duty. It is customary nowadays to emphasize that the secular tradition, in poetry, in philosophy and so on, was never wholly lost; that the common man, so far as we are able to trace out and listen to his views, was by no means as orthodox in his religious opinions as some have hopefully pretended; that mediaeval culture was an uneasy coalition of Christian, Greco-Roman, barbarian and other values; and that the state began to emerge as a second great power-centre rivalling the church as early as the twelfth century.[6] Nevertheless, the generalization still holds: for about twelve centuries the pursuit of truth was simply identified with the work of building up and defending the Christian order. Not only the church, but the whole culture remained ultimately subject to the spiritual hierarchy, whose power was truth. The propagation of unauthorized religious opinions was a threat to the controlling truth-power, and was punishable by death.

How did the will to truth and the will to maintain the Christian social order ever become separated from each other? Explanations of many different kinds can be put forward. Historians may speak about the growth of the civil power, of trade and of cities, and the gradual emergence of consciously-secular spheres of life. Others may see in the Italian renaissance a growing spirit of individualism that passes continuously through the painters and sculptors to the engineers and architects, and then to the medical men, mathematicians and natural philosophers. A rather different type of explanation was offered by Newman, who blamed Luther for letting loose the spirit of 'subjective rationalism'. At the Diet of Worms in 1521 Luther had put forward quite explicitly a new criterion of religious truth: what conscience is impelled to believe on reading scripture is true, whatever the church may say.[7] By thus driving a wedge between 'what scripture says' and 'what the present-day church teaches', Luther created a conflict between two different touchstones of religious truth. After he had set scripture and tradition in opposition to each other, it could no longer simply be assumed uncritically that the active defence of the established Christian social and religious order by the church was *eo ipso* the promotion of the truth. But once this question of the touchstone of truth had been raised, it was soon found that there was no easy way to resolve it. Critical study of scripture and early church history began, with one party attempting to prove the continuity of scripture and the Catholic system, and the other their discontinuity. The controversy has never been finally laid to rest since; and the question of the touchstone of truth soon spread beyond the religious sphere. People asked, by what criterion can we test, not merely religious knowledge, but knowledge in general?

Again the question, once raised, could never be laid to rest. The scepticism of the ancients was revived. Critical thinking, and indeed the entire tradition of modern philosophy up to the present day, has been dominated by the attempt to overcome scepticism. What we have learned about the nature of our knowledge-systems during these three or four centuries has been enough to ensure that the old alliance between the will to truth and the will to maintain the social order can never again be restored with quite the old unconscious confidence. A repressive state may seek legitimation from Marxist philosophy, but since Marxism is a species of *critical* philosophy it cannot but be aware of how it is being used, and this awareness introduces an element of bad conscience into the alliance which must eventually lead to its dissolution.

An interesting psychological explanation of the rise of an autonomous will to truth is offered by Nietzsche and Foucault, though its ultimate source doubtless lies in Hegel. According to this account, knowledge works as a tool of power, and knowledge-systems are elaborated in order to augment the power of those who possess the knowledge. In the history of human sciences such as penology, psychiatry, medicine and so forth we observe that his initiation into a body of professional lore equips the professional with a set of tools that he uses to probe and to control the motives, the secret thoughts and the behaviour of his clients. In describing this phenomenon we readily invoke the metaphors of *priesthood, sacred text, orthodoxy, inquisition, heresy* and the like, which reminds us that many of the more recently-developed knowledge systems resemble the theology of former times. It was in precisely the periods when the claims of church authority were pitched highest that theology became most highly elaborate and objectified. Canon law, dogmatic theology and moral theology were the cleric's professional equipment. The more refined the regulation of conduct, the definition of heresy and the analysis of the roots of sin became, the more searchingly the church could extend its control over the behaviour, the thought, and the inner life of the laity.

So far, so obvious. We are reminded of Disraeli's finger-wagging admonition to a lax church dignitary: liberal views are all very well but, 'remember, Mr Dean: no dogma, no Dean!' But now the analysis becomes more interesting. The penitent who undergoes interrogation by these powerful and searching instruments is himself changed by them. He becomes introspective and troubled about the state of his own soul. He experiences an intensification of self-awareness or subjectivity. Like the young Luther, he may borrow the tools which the confessor has used upon him, and use them upon himself in his scrupulous search for inner integrity and truthfulness. In this way he discovers for himself the use and power of the tools, how obscure and tangled human motives are, how hard it is ever to come to rest in the truth, and how deeply-divided the tools either make the self, or show it to be. But now his heightened self-consciousness, his scepticism and his knowledge of how to use the tools suggest to him that he may find a solution by using the tools back against the institution that first awakened him by using them upon him. So the will to truth, the demythol-ogizing, sceptical and enquiring spirit, develops when a knowledge-power system goes too far, overreaches itself and provokes a retaliatory reaction against itself. It has inadvertently armed its victim.

There are many modern parallels. Psychoanalysis is notoriously liable to produce a retaliatory reaction of this kind. The tools it used upon the client equip the client to seize them and use them back against it. Perhaps that *is* the cure. A case much discussed in recent literature is that of homosexuality. A traditionally patriar-chal society was confronted at the end of the nineteenth century by the threat of female emancipation. In order to defend the traditional order, male psychologists invented a large number of new concepts defining various forms of deviation from the sexual norm.[8] They were intended as tools to make people ashamed of themselves and bring them back into line, and for a while they worked as such. But in time people came to accept the novel idea that they really were to be defined as persons in terms of their sexual orientation, and used it to fight back with Gay Liberation movements and the like.

Finally, an example which caused much irritation and amuse-ment when it first appeared not long ago; the case of the Educated Prisoner. The state bodies concerned with operating the penal system have over the years employed sociologists to develop a body of criminological theory which explains in causal language why crimes are committed and suggests how to reduce them. The theory was developed on behalf of the state and as an instrument of social control, but since learned publication is in the vernacular and prisoners may occupy their enforced leisure with courses of study in the social sciences, it is not surprising that some Prisoners' Rights groups have appropriated the intellectual tools developed to explain and control their own behaviour, and have used those tools on their own behalf back against the system.

Can an analysis of this kind be carried through in the case of physical science? Governments evidently regard scientific knowledge as a form of power and encourage its growth; and professional communities of scientists evidently do behave in some ways like priesthoods, generating and defending an orthodox consensus and promoting their own cause. On the other hand, you cannot quite *see through* physical science as a power-ideology in the same way as you can *see through* most other bodies of knowledge. People do not come out of it comprehensively dissillusioned with it in the same way as they may come out disillusioned from an ideological group. You cannot use physics back against itself. It seems therefore that physical science partly or largely escapes ideological analysis. But it only escapes insofar as it is not in the business of giving 'meaning' to life by generating that special sense of a moral reality to inhabit and moral goals to seek that human communities need to live by. If it gives us almost the only objective knowledge we have, it does so only at the price of *not* giving us the meaning we seek, and so its ability to rescue us from our present cultural crisis is zero. Indeed it worsens the crisis, for it works as a powerful demystifying agent, dissolving away traditional sources of 'meaning' and putting nothing in their place, especially when it starts explaining *us* and making us sceptical about the very concepts by which we understand ourselves.

At the opposite extreme from this lie religious knowledge-systems, where the ability to give 'meaning' to life is at its greatest and the element of objective knowledge is at its least. It is here that the power-analysis is most obviously applicable – and nowadays people know it. Increasingly, small religious communities of every kind, evangelical, charismatic, pentecostal and revivalist, cults, consciousness-raising movements and religious orders, are divided into two classes of people. There is a small cadre of permanent professionals who are in it for power, and a much larger class of mainly younger people who stay in the group for between two and five years or thereabouts. Disoriented and dispossessed converts joining the group are very glad to accept the group's power over them in exchange for the 'meaning' it gives them. They are often most attracted to the most authoritarian groups, as if they already half-recognize the principle that the more authoritarian the group, the more meaning it gives, but they do not balk at it. They throw themselves enthusiastically into the system; but the more it penetrates *them* the better they understand *it*, and therefore, inevitably, they begin to see through it. After a few years they come to the parting of the ways. They must change their relation to the system, either joining the permanent cadre or leaving. The permanent cadre is well-satisfied if it can recruit about a tenth of those who pass through, and thus slowly increase its own numbers. As for those who leave, they have learnt a useful lesson and gained something in consciousness and freedom. In some cultures today there are individuals who go into, through and out of several such groups, one after another. They are the true romantics, who continue to hope that the kind of 'meaning' they are looking for can be had apart from the kind of power-system that they cannot help seeing through. But it cannot – and that is our crisis. We are very reluctant to accept that the disenchanted critical consciousness that has been developed in us by the failure of our search for objective meaningfulness may *itself* be the only kind of 'meaning' now available to us. So we continue to look outwards rather than inwards, nostalgically searching for a kind of meaningfulness in life which we believe used to exist, which we think essential, and which we desperately hope can in some way be restored. But there is now implanted within us that critical demon which ensures that we will repeatedly disillusion ourselves. Indeed people had (or thought they had) objective meaningfulness in traditional societies, but the invention of the concept of myth and other changes that occurred at the time of the Enlightenment have made a return to traditional ways of thinking impossible. Those who still defend the remnants of tradition do so with arguments that look more and more sceptical, and from motives that look more and more openly political. The drift to naked authoritarianism in all this is even more apparent in the various new ways to meaning currently on offer in the cultural market-place. Every last one of them confirms our growing suspicion that the sort of meaningfulness we seek, and which we persistently fancy it the proper business of religion to provide, can nowadays only be created by a power-ideology such as sooner or later we cannot help seeing through. The larger-scale political scene shows a similar contradiction, polarized as it is between free societies full of spiritual *anomie* and internal conflict, and ideological tyrannies in which social life seems superficially more peaceable and purposive, but which can never wholly suppress the voice of critical questioning that threatens to topple them.

Must we not conclude from all this that the ancient habit of looking for meaning to a socially-established objective authority must now be given up? There is no way that social religion can work any longer. It is time to change our very concept of religion. But old habits die hard: people's sense of reality, their sense of being in the truth, still depends on the strength of the public moral order. Consider, for example, how in fiction *naturalism is moralism*: that is, in a naturalistic novel the clarity and stability of the novelist's picture of human nature and social relations depends upon the strength of the moral framework within which he (the novelist) sets them. I have in mind here books like *Middlemarch* and *Anna Karenina*. Today, however, we cannot see how the public moral order can be re-established in a form that will stand up to critical questioning. In the British tradition, G. E. Moore produced in his *Principia Ethica* (1903) a classical argument, the so-called 'naturalistic fallacy', which sought to prove in quite general terms that any attempt to give morality an objective foundation in facts about God or the world or human nature must contain a fallacy.[9] By now his argument has itself been very thoroughly criticized,[10] but nevertheless it still marks a watershed, and all attempts to restore objectivity by appealing to intuition or rational consistency or by returning to Aristotle have themselves been extensively criticized in their turn. Nietzsche, who sees all these issues with exceptional clarity, asks, 'Why do we *want* there to be objective meaningfulness? Why not just *pull out*?',[11] and he returns to a position like that of Thrasymachus in Plato's *Republic*: the only remaining basis for morality is the creative self-affirmation of the strong individual who disciplines his desires. The will of the strong is the ultimate source of moral value. But there is an element of inconsistency in Nietzsche himself, for the nihilistic side of his philosophy really leaves no objective guidelines either without us or within us, but only a complete blank. On that side of his thinking he can see only the end of the world, a universal conflagration, and no reason at all for constructing any one new reality rather than any other. But the other side of Nietzsche's philosophy is a form of biological naturalism; and here there are, he thinks, some ultimate facts about the world and human nature which make it appropriate to will the creation of one particular new reality rather than some other. Nietzsche's inconsistency lies in the fact that he uses the nihilistic side of his thinking to persuade us that the end of the old world has come, and then draws upon the naturalistic side of his thinking to take us through it and give us a glimpse of what may lie on the far side – 'saying Yes to life'.

Nietzsche justified the naturalistic side of his thinking by his metaphysics of the will-to-power. Critical analysis shows that all human cultural products and social life can be reduced to transforms of our instinctual drives and passions. Continuing the analysis, Nietzsche next reduces the natural world to a plurality of energy-quanta, point wills-to-power each striving to extend its power. A living organism is a confederacy of these atomic centres of struggle-for-power. Thus Nietzsche's sceptical analysis demythologizes away until nothing is left but will-to-power, free to create whatever moral reality is most fitting for it.[12]

However, the metaphysics of the will-to-power may itself be regarded as yet one more rationalization, a fiction devised for the strong to justify their own self-affirmation and to suggest to them the form it should take. On his constructive side, Nietzsche is still at the old game of inventing a metaphysic to justify an ethic. He would have been more consistent, and he would have prevented the subsequent abuse of his philosophy by political demagogues, if he had stuck more closely to pure nihilism. His message would then have been simply that the critical principle of the will-to-truth, once released, is unstoppable. Dissolving the moral world away entirely, it will also undermine every attempt to reconstitute it. On the good side, this means that no tyranny can stand against it, but on the bad side it reduces us to a peculiarly naked and dreadful condition of isolated, contentless freedom, with all bearings lost. The young Hume admirably described this condition,[13] and it has been made the starting-point for various existentialist philosophies. Our argument has suggested that it is a return in modern guise of the eschatological crisis out of which the Christian message first arose, and that in order to get through it we have to make the transition that Christianity at first hoped to make, from social religion to the Kingdom of God.

Is the parallel sound? It may be objected that Jesus predicted the supernaturally-caused dissolution of the entire cosmos, which is scarcely the issue today. However, the primary meaning of the word 'world', then as now, was the *milieu*, the 'age' or the cultural totality within which human life is lived. In this sense we speak of Shakespeare's world or the age of Rembrandt, and we have in mind not merely the manners of the period but the entire socially-constructed reality of that time with all its metaphysical and moral assumptions. Such a world may come to an end, now as then; and because the common-sense physical world about us and the more refined world of natural science are both of them constructed from within the social world, a major transformation of the social world leads to a corresponding change in the perceived physical world. A new society means a new earth and a new heaven. And in the second place, since the primary and social world is a *moral* order, to proclaim its end is to urge moral change. A prophet who pronounced judgment upon a city was not merely issuing a forecast; he was urging repentance and the establishment of a new moral reality. He perceived contradictions within the present moral world which would lead to its destruction unless people's outlook and behaviour underwent a radical change. However, the greater the change that the prophet calls for, the more impossible it is to understand him. Language so embeds me in this world that 'the world and life are one. I am my world . . . the limits of language (the language which I understand) mean the limits of my world.'[14] The end of my moral world, in which I am thus completely embedded, presents me with the same impassable limit as my own death. There is no way of envisaging a 'beyond' because at the limit, 'the world does not change, but ceases'.[15] So the prophet is bound to be understood as talking about the end of the world, and he is obliged to eke out his message by borrowing from mythology and talking about the restoration of the primal time of perfection, or about death and rebirth. Alternatively, he may do deliberate violence to meanings by way of trying to forge a new language to describe the new reality, or, most subtly, he may seek surreptitiously to feed in new meanings by the use of irony.

If he does this latter with some success, there may arise a

situation where the new world and new order of meaning has established a bridgehead in the old world, but neither replaces it nor succumbs to it. The two worlds of meaning overlap and coexist in a strange mixture of alliance and conflict. The culture becomes permanently ironical. People allude almost compulsively to their awareness that the way they live makes sense in terms of one world but is absurd by the standards of the other.

Much of the Christian tradition so far has been like this, but Britain is surely the country which in modern times has had the most highly ironical culture. On the one hand it is the country in which the political theory of possessive individualism was developed by Hobbes, Locke and their successors, and in which normality is chronic conflict between egoistic interest-groups in all areas of public life; and yet on the other hand people also profess to despise the riches, fame and honours that they seek, and play the world's game only in the hope of one day being able to get out of it. And the philanthropic and altruistic tradition remains remarkably strong. Perhaps the most impressive example of it is the voluntary blood donor. Richard Titmuss points out how markedly the gift of one's own blood in modern Britain contrasts with gifts in traditional societies:

> (In) the free gift of blood to unnamed strangers there is no formal contract, no legal bond, no situation of power, domination, constraint or compulsion, no sense of shame or guilt, no gratitude imperative, no need for penitence, no money and no explicit guarantee of or wish for a reward or a return gift.[16]

The phenomenon is modern, for blood-groups were discovered only in 1901, and the National Blood Transfusion Service was established only in 1948. The donors are broadly representative of the general population, with a slight bias towards the young and the male. Religious motives are not thought to be especially prominent.[17]

This behaviour flatly contradicts the pessimistic assumption, made by both conservative theologians and economists, that the natural man is a rational egoist. By 1968 the ever-growing number of donors had reached 1.44 millions. Here is a practical demonstration, on a scale and in a purity for which there can be few historical precedents, that altruism is possible and can be given effective institutional expression. It belies the popular charge that the ethic of the Kingdom of God is 'impractical', for Titmuss demonstrated that the British system works much better than the American. And it works in a culture which is 'decadent', 'bourgeois', 'capitalist' and all the rest.

Titmuss argued that the makers of social policy must not simply assume an egoistic model of human nature in all the provisions they make, but should so arrange things as to foster the spirit of altruism so that it can slowly increase its scope and raise the quality of life. In a rather secular idiom, he was reaffirming a traditional Christian hope: admittedly the two worlds now co-exist very awkwardly, but the new world whose moral order will be based on the principle of pure disinterested gift does have a foothold among us, and if we act intelligently and allow it to grow and extend itself it may gradually displace the old dying order.

Such a gradualist approach has seemed to many to be implied in a number of Jesus' parables, and it played an important part in the doctrine of the church taught by liberal theology. What is wrong with it, and why go so far as to suggest that a revolutionary rather than a gradual transformation is now imperative? There are various considerations. Marxist criticism has suggested that Christian moral idealism does not really ameliorate, but rather is cunningly exploited by, a social reality which is more powerful, more antagonistic and more shrewd than it innocently supposes. In return for being permitted a limited number of outlets, it is used to validate and strengthen the forces which it naively hoped to transform. Changing tack in response to this criticism, Christian gradualism may seek instead to ally itself with the optimistic and progressive humanist movements that emerged especially in the 1840s. Could it not swim with that tide and make a final, transforming contribution to its eventual goal? But since those heady days the secular picture and prospect has become darker and darker, as people have digested the implications of the teaching of Darwin, Nietzsche, Freud and others. The public moral order has decayed so far that it has been said that morally-speaking we are like survivors in a severely polluted world who go from town to town searching out and looting the remaining scattered stocks of canned food and drink. Not having any nourishing common vision of the good for man, nor any agreed criteria for settling moral disputes, we are obliged to live from hand to mouth by picking up the available fragments of various former moralities and using them as best we can. We are not self-sustaining any more, and find ourselves having to live off scraps from the past, because we are no longer able rationally to justify moral beliefs before any generally-acknowledged public tribunal.

Alasdair MacIntyre, describing our present condition in these terms,[18] argues that the choice now lies between Aristotle and Nietzsche. He rejects Nietzsche's own strange mixture of apocalyptic and barbarism, because he holds that it is still possible to construct a rational foundation for morality along Aristotle's lines. At least in small communities, a rational vision of the good life and the practice of the virtues may be maintained through the dark times that have already come upon us.

This is not an easy undertaking, for unless some contrary view can actually be *proved*, Nietzsche will always win the argument by default. For the task remains what it has always been: how do you convince the strong and self-reliant individual who can look after himself and does not give a damn that it is rational for him consistently to accept the restraints of justice, to his own disadvantage? Suppose we join Nietzsche and look at morals genealogically: the old public moral order, never very coherent, has broken down and the time of the barbarians has come. The will of the strong is the only law. They enforce a new moral order which expresses their prowess and their careless pride. In time, though, their ascendancy provokes *ressentiment* among the lower classes. Feeling builds up until there is a slave revolt and the moral order is transformed. Pride and strength become shameful, and instead men are equal in their subjection to a universal moral law which is backed up with various fictions. But when the severe demands of this new moral order make themselves felt in people's souls, they successively give rise to conscience, troubled individual subjectivity, and the will to truth. Thus the plebeian moral order creates forces which begin to eat away at it from within. It dissolves, breaks down, and the barbarian rulers return to begin a fresh cycle. So it goes and goes, for ever.

Nietzsche can endure this futile circle, for it is compatible with his point of view. But his opponents cannot endure it, and the onus is on them to show that they can break out of it and establish an indestructibly secure order. Taking up the challenge, MacIntyre rejects the whole modern tradition of individualism that culminated in Nietzsche, and returns to Aristotle. The task is to restate the best Greek view of social life, of human well-being and the virtues, without calling upon the now-dead teleological biology that Aristotle himself relied upon. But Nietzschean scepticism cuts and undercuts away remorselessly: in developing his argument MacIntyre has to invoke ideas of rationality, of human life as potentially a meaningful story, of a stable human character, of the good for man, and of the moral precedence of society over the individual – and Nietzsche can reject all such ideas as convenient ideological fictions that are produced, hold firm for a while, and then bring about their own unmasking by the working out of their own inner logic. Once again the sceptical, critical, debunking spirit of the will to truth, driving towards nihilism, seems able to dissolve into a phantom every opponent that steps forward to bar its way.

Perhaps Nietzsche cannot be stopped; perhaps the only way to turn the tables upon him is to seize his own weapons, direct them against him, and go even further than he does himself. He has said that we must give up every sort of 'idealism' that tries to pretend that things are other than they really are, and then uses this pretence to back up an attempt to force things to be other than they are. He has shown how every sort of moral order by which men have sought to live – with the exception of the one briefly glimpsed at the beginning of Christianity – has been either openly or in a sneaky and indirect way a tool of domination, and he has shown how it brings about its own dissolution by the working out of its own logic. So let us use that insight to reject his own metaphysics of the will-to-power, *amor fati*, the eternal recurrence, and the Superman, as being themselves products of his own wishful thinking, a sick man's dream of health and strength, a dream that cannot be realized. Let us give up every last trace of the belief that a viable public moral order can be constructed either by philosophical reasoning or by the will's own self-affirmation. A whole way of thinking has simply come to an end.

Nietzsche, who misses little, has seen this possibility. He calls it 'passive nihilism'. Since he believes that nothing else exists in reality but will-to-power and its various transformations and expressions, the renunciation of even will-to-power leaves him facing a pure blank from which he recoils in horror. He describes this absolute nihilism as the product of exhaustion, failure, sickness and pessimism. But this over-excited language is quite inappropriate. If we must coolly set aside any wish or expectation that things should be other than they are, and if there is nothing other than *this* by contrast with which *this* can be characterized, then romantic attitudes of defiance or despair and talk of passive nihilism are irrelevant, for they presuppose an illusory contrast. It would be more appropriate to wait upon the ultimate truth of the human condition with a quiet and unflinching gaze, like a traditional monk meditating upon a skull until all egoistic illusions of possession and domination had been burnt out of him by what he saw.

Nietzsche could see what absolute nihilism was, but he lacked the religious discipline to wait with it long enough to see the possibility of salvation on the far side of it. He sensed an affinity between the will to truth and the ascetical quest, but instead of following it through he spent his efforts on (no doubt well-deserved) polemics against the pathological side of religion. He would not see that the best ascetical tradition had been just as keen as he to discard destructive images of God, morbid psychology and consolatory illusions of every kind, and more keen than he to follow the way of negation to the very end.

Where does it lead? Let us press on. It is quite possible, and indeed it is the case with us, that the natural sciences may flourish and that small-scale diminutions of human unhappiness can be and are achieved, while yet at a deeper level people's sense of reality is disintegrating. Critical doubts about the foundations of morals and about the possibility of establishing any public moral order lead towards nihilism. Some would retreat to traditional dogmatic certainties, but such certainties are merely tribal, none is universal, none can stand up to lengthy interrogation, and the retreat to them leads to destructive conflict. Progress can only be made in the *opposite* direction, by following a path like that outlined in various systems of meditation, Eastern and Western.[19] Push on with the critical questioning, and let the dissolution of all internal and external structures take its course. When the self and the world become completely deconstructed, egoism is uprooted. Only pure, undifferentiated and objectless awareness remains: the ego has lost internal structure. There is no longer anything *there* that is anxious for itself or that might attempt to assert itself

by domination or by projecting and imposing its own ordered
self-expression upon the world.

In this way passive nihilism leads to a condition of complete
inner loss. For an individual to pass through this experience is for
him to die a little inside, as if he had suffered a very close
bereavement, or passed through a severe mental breakdown or an
illness expected to be fatal. Any new lease of life on the far side is
a pure bonus. What it might be for a whole community to pass
through this experience I cannot say, though we may learn in the
next few decades. At any rate, on returning to the everyday world,
all experience is seen as pure gift. No lien can be claimed upon it,
and there is no longer any motive for harbouring illusory expectations or taking anything as of right and for granted. It is in this
strange new condition that a new kind of moral reality emerges.

For reasons already given, it is not easy to describe except in
negative terms. All previous moralities have already come to be
seen as created by egoism, anxiety, and the will to dominate.
Whether directly or indirectly, they have been attempts forcibly
to impose an order, and to seek the security of an objective ground
of meaning against which we can measure ourselves and others in
order to establish everyone's relative status. In all human relationships there has been an element of domination: a superior and an
inferior in worth, a creditor and a debtor, a giver and a receiver.
Now the world is swept clean of all such ideas. Nothing prevents
or occludes simple sociality, disinterestedness, altruism: there is
a kind of spontaneous generation of value. But so corrupt are our
language and ways of thinking that it is most difficult to imagine
love and justice apart from the exercise of power. For example,
some represent the ethic of the Kingdom of God as an active
willing of the neighbour's good, which immediately suggests to us
that it is merely a sublimated form of the old will to dominate. I
form a picture of what would be good for my neighbour, and
begin to manoeuvre him towards it. That cannot be right, for a
truly disinterested love can neither seek recognition nor seek to
change its object. Even object-*choice* is already somewhat dubious, for it implies a singling out for special attention and,
probably, pressure. And if we turn to the concept of justice, it is
equally hard to think away power-ideas, for we inevitably begin
with an image of an authoritative and impartial referee who
ensures that all get fair shares, that contracts are fulfilled and

rights respected, and so on. We assume a picture of human beings as basically aggressive and competitive, but reasoning themselves into appointing a referee. It is so difficult to imagine real human relationships without the power factor, that when we try to remove it we seem to imagine a rather loose association of individuals who each quietly radiate, but do not really engage with each other. As we now see things, the will-to-power is necessary in order to give substance to human relations. God himself seemed more real in the days when he was an uncompromisingly commanding will-to-power over the believer; the coming God of powerless love seems to us insubstantial by comparison.

Yet difficult though it inevitably is to imagine the ethic of the Kingdom of God, we have some inkling of it. Altruism does exist; we have mentioned blood-donors as an example of it. The old belief that it may be possible to pass through the fire to a new kind of moral world has never wholly died, and has some evidence in its support. If we have come to a time when what I have called social religion has finally died, and carried off with it any chance of reconstructing the older kind of moral order, then very soon the new world will have to be chosen. The message of religion is that in the end it is the only possibility.

9

THE NEW WORLD

Although the main argument is complete, we are still left with a number of important questions of meaning.

To begin with, there is the common complaint that revisionist theologies are not less but more obscure and uncertain in content than the traditional realist faith they purport to replace. For example, one of the last prolific and popular authors to commend an uncompromisingly supernaturalist theology was C. S. Lewis. Now it must be conceded at once that Lewis's world-view had many unpleasing aspects. It seldom really comes to life either imaginatively or as religion, except in the late pseudonymous book *A Grief Observed*, and Lewis's self-conscious rejection of modernity leads him close to vindictiveness on the many occasions when he arranges supernatural retribution for people and points of view that he dislikes. There is all too much holy relish. But at least Lewis wrote well. People feel they understand him, reckon they can see what difference it would make to come to hold his views, and regard him as typical of mainstream Christianity. Like it or not, he stands for something recognizable, whereas – or so we are told – the revisionist theologies are often strange, unfamiliar and hard to identify as Christian, and so ambiguous that it is not at all clear what *difference* they make.

However, these charges usually reflect an expectation that has been disappointed because it is mistaken. The mistake is that of supposing that what is at issue is merely a *doctrinal* shift from one sort of realist theology to another. Not so: the real shift is *philosophical*. Our perception of religious meaning is undergoing profound change. The place where it is to be found is shifting from tradition and external authority to individual subjectivity, and as a result it is leaving the metaphysical domain and becoming concentrated in the domain of ethics and spirituality. Religious meaning is becoming less a matter of metaphysical facts and more a matter of insights and ideals that are discovered to be illuminating, life-guiding and life-transforming. This process has been going on irregularly for centuries and is now reaching completion. Its upshot is that Christianity has now to be seen not as a body of supernatural facts certified to us by various authorities and evidences, but as a body of ideals and practices that have the power to give ultimate worth to human life. If this thesis is correct, then it is a misunderstanding to judge a radical theology in terms of whether it strays beyond the permitted limits of orthodoxy, or in terms of its realist metaphysical content. The whole thesis is that the very idea of the juridical control of religious thought from above makes no sense any more, and that the very idea that religious beliefs express theories about invisible beings must now be seen as a category-mistake. That being so, it is question-begging to disregard the theologian's argument and insist on judging what he says by criteria that he rejects and has not attempted to meet. When he has argued at length that all the assumptions behind the traditional concept of heresy are mistaken, it is a trifle obtuse merely to dismiss him as a heretic.

Certainly religious meaning is a most mysterious and elusive thing. It can seem at one time to be present, solid and indubitable, and then only a little later to have unexpectedly withdrawn itself and melted away. Idioms that once seemed clearly intelligible and authoritative can lose their power and go dead on us, and we scarcely know why it has happened. And there can be no doubt that this is happening today to large areas of traditional religious language. It is simply no longer clear what (if anything) is being said and what (if any) claim is being made. People say that a revised version of religious belief is a waste of time if nothing intelligible is being said, and I accept the point and will try to meet it; but by the same token religious conservatism is also a waste of time if the heart has gone out of it and there is nothing left to conserve. Why seek the living among the dead?

Some such loss of meaning appears to have happened recently to Dr Billy Graham, at any rate in relation to his British audiences. In 1980 at Oxford the loss was so painfully apparent that some of his ardent young Evangelical supporters, who had been expecting such great things of his Mission there, lost their faith.[1] Noting and analysing some of his sermons that spring, I was startled by their lack of religious content. The words were much the same as ever, but somehow there was nothing in them any more. Nor is Dr Graham in any way exceptional in this, for many highly-respected figures of the older generation who speak a religious language formed in the 'fifties or earlier have suffered the same fate, often without realizing it. Others, who have become aware of their own language's increasing hollowness, are tempted to envy them their innocence.

The disintegration of the old comprehensive realist theology is particularly well illustrated in Britain by the reports of successive Doctrine Commissions of the Church of England. In 1938 a Commission chaired by William Temple had issued a very successful report.[2] It was systematic in form, and was agreed by all members without dissent. It showed traditional doctrine undergoing modification and diversification but nonetheless remaining coherent, and liberal too. It was reprinted in 1962 at a time of theological upheaval. Naturally many people wanted to see the political-dogmatic coherence and social authority of Anglican teaching reaffirmed, and hoped that Temple's achievement could be repeated in the new conditions a generation after the War. A distinguished group was appointed, but its Report in 1976[3] contained no agreed systematic statement. The Joint Report and ten individual signed contributions were all devoted to expressing and ruminating upon the difference between those who think in terms of an unchanging supernatural Faith and those who think in terms of a continual quest for new formulations of faith in response to historical change; and the latter group appeared to have the best of the argument. This was not good enough, and the discontent was compounded when next year three members of the Commission appeared among the contributors to *The Myth of God Incarnate*. The Commission was dissolved, and subsequently a new and supposedly safer body was established. It was again hoped that now at last we would see limits drawn, deviations rejected and mainline doctrine systematically reaffirmed. But these expectations were confounded when the 1981 Report[4] proved to be more cautious than ever. It contained no Joint Statement at all, but only individually signed essays. Out went the politically unacceptable term 'myth', and in came its innocuous synonym 'story'. There were some remarks aimed at marginalizing the radicals, religious individualism was rebuked, and we were reminded that faith is corporate and theologians have a respon-sibility to the community they serve. But all this was mere political exhortation, of no specifically religious value. It bore an uncanny resemblance to the ineffectual pleadings currently being addressed to the British Labour Party by its leader Michael Foot, and the restoration of an agreed body of clear-cut doctrine around which the faithful could rally to attack the enemy seemed as far off in the one case as the other. After two attempts in a single decade it had proved impossible, with the best will in the world, to produce the kind of confident semi-official statement of realist doctrine that so many people craved. Somehow conditions had changed, and what could still be done in the pre-War years could no longer be done today.

Why is this? Essentially it is because the ancient connection between truth and social authority has at last broken down. Doctrine was able to be objective, coherent and systematic only so long as that connection held. But critical thinking erodes the connection and shows another path to truth, until eventually a time comes when the old link between truth and social authority ceases even to be intelligible. We can no longer even understand how the authorities in a certain community can fully possess the whole truth, the absolute and ultimately-important truth, not as the result of any special research or critical enquiry whatever but *merely by virtue of the office they hold*, or how they can possess juridical authority to determine and enforce truth, or how they can actually create belief by authoritative proclamation so that all members of the community shall come to understand and profess just the same faith in the same way. Of course, we can well understand that Stalin was able to make Lysenko's biology *dominant* in Soviet science, but we do not understand how any exercise of power on Stalin's part could actually have made Lysenko's biology *true*; and correspondingly we can well imagine that religious conservatism may become dominant in a church and then legislate to enforce its own views, but this would be a merely political occurrence. There is no way that we can under-stand how the mere exertion of power can genuinely convert bad arguments into sound ones or restore religious meaning to idioms that have lost it. If the issue be put in more moderate terms, and the determination of religious truth be seen as a matter of the consent of the faithful established by polling or through some kind of Synod or Council, even so, that one party should prevail or secure a majority for its views is still only a political fact and cannot of itself settle the question of truth. The 1981 Doctrine Report just referred to unfortunately often speaks as if the slowly-evolving consent of the faithful is the highest criterion of religious truth; but if it is, then current religious doctrine is no more than a function of current fashion, and is not true by the standards that the surrounding culture requires. For in our culture there is only one path to real truth. There is not much real truth, and it is only provisional; but it is all we have, and it is found by the rigorous testing of theories against evidence not under their control, by free critical reason operating *independently* of social authority. That alone is truth, and everything else is the product of power, fashion, custom and choice.

Suppose we wish to know what is meant by the resurrection of Christ. We may study the arguments (not the conclusions so much as the *arguments*) of scholars like Schillebeeckx with profit. But what can it *mean* to say that a group of Roman canonists, who know little of the niceties of theological debate, have such a special supernatural knowledge of the meaning of resurrection-talk that they are entitled to call Schillebeeckx to account, correct him and so on?[5] Indeed in the case in question they claimed supernatural expertise in philosophy, for they claimed to have authority to pronounce upon such questions as what is to be meant by speaking of 'the objective reality' of the resurrection. It is sometimes mistakenly thought that liberal and radical theologians *resent* the determination of truth by power, but the truth is rather that we do not *understand* it. We recognize that power may be used to enforce a law, but how can power settle questions of truth?

At the time of writing the final outcome of the Schillebeeckx affair is still in doubt; but those at Rome who are politically aware will need no reminding of the dangers of ever invoking the Pope's power to legislate autonomously in matters of faith and morals. The dilemma is simple: unless the Pope uses arguments he cannot persuade, but if he does then he inevitably lays himself open to counter-arguments. So in the end only arguments count, and not authority. The fate of the Encyclical *Humanae Vitae* (1967) showed the way the wind is blowing. It used arguments, but at the point that matters, the point where arguments are weighed in the individual conscience, they were found not to be telling. Here was a sign of the way in which in recent decades religious meaning has finally slipped the leash and escaped from the old authoritative controls. It now belongs to individuals.

In this connection some sociologists speak of the modern privatization of religion,[6] first foreshadowed in Tom Paine's 'My mind is my church', and Jefferson's 'I am a sect myself'. They mean that we are now so diversified as persons, so autonomous in our thinking about the ultimate questions of life, and so committed to seeing the religious task as the working-out of a personal view of life and the path to individuation, that nowadays each of us must in effect evolve his own religion for himself. And this is true even for members of the most traditional churches. For example, if we study the work of a dozen well-known Catholic novelists, we find that their differences from one another, as they each work out his or her own view of life, are far more significant than what they have in common. What they have in common – the apparatus of Catholic doctrine, symbolism and practice – provides them with useful stage-properties and imaginative resources, but it is used only instrumentally in the working out of what in everything that really matters are very disparate imaginative worlds. So it is with each one of us. We all inevitably and rightly make instrumental use of traditional materials, but in the end each of us has to seek and test religious meaning for himself in the only remaining proving-ground, our own personal experience of life and our own subjectivity. As R. N. Bellah puts it, the trend of modern religious development is not towards indifference and secularization but towards 'increasing acceptance of the notion that each individual must work out his own ultimate solutions and that the most the church can do is provide him with a favourable environment for doing so, without imposing on him a prefabricated set of answers'.[7]

History has ingrained in us a habit of looking to higher authority to create meaning, to define truth and to lay down the limits of what is permissible in religion. The Father-knows-best view of life finds it hard to envisage any mean between on the one hand monarchical rule and peaceful ideological *sobornost* (the obedient unanimity of the gathered faithful), and on the other hand mere anarchy, subjectivism run riot. But Bellah is not suggesting that religious associations are likely to disappear altogether: rather, he thinks that we shall see the emergence of a new kind of flexible, innovative and creative religious organization. The old kind of church discouraged creativity on principle, describing it as heresy. The new kind will be 'heretical' through-and-through. It will *have* to be so, for the will to truth requires it. Until the seventeenth century it was believed that meaning came down from heaven, and that language itself was supernatural, for it had first been taught to men by God. God was the first and prime language-user, his word created and his word written being the supreme texts for men to study. Language was charged with supernatural authority, powers and meanings greater than men could understand. But since the time of Thomas Hobbes[8] it has come to be realized that language evolved from below and was created by men. Man is the maker of meaning: all the vast range of human cultural institutions and activities have come to be seen as human social products, and this includes all the various ideologies that have been evolved to conceal the human origins of institutions. Hence modern anthropocentrism; and it presents us not with a new task, but with the challenge to perform an old task in a new and clearer consciousness of its nature. It is not that meaning used really to come down from above, whereas now we have the new task of generating it from below. It is that meaning always *was* generated from below, but now we know it, and so will henceforth be unable to use the traditional self-mystifying devices. Religious meaning used to be created by projecting fictions, forgetting their character, and then falling under their spell. Human life was made tolerable, was indeed greatly enriched, by a marvellously ingenious social mechanism of self-enchantment. Now we know how the trick was done, and we cannot work the spell upon ourselves in quite the old way. We have to become clear-eyed and active generators of religious meaning; and this is what I mean by the move to the Third Age, the age of the Spirit, or the Kingdom of God.

However, I am still fearful lest I make the shift appear too easy. It is not. How difficult it is to make may be brought out by contrasting the situation in Christianity with that in certain old and easy-going oriental faiths.

In India we often find a distinction made between popular

religious practice and the higher teachings. It is tolerantly recognized that those whose lives are hardest and most insecure will always tend to see religion as a way of securing their own well-being and averting misfortune. The ordinary man's religion is eudaemonistic. He sees himself as surrounded by powerful hidden spirit-beings who control his fate, and he needs their favour. Like a city storekeeper in the USA, he thinks that in a dangerous world it makes sense to pay dues to a godfather; and since his religion is about his own survival, he fancies that the spirit-beings are just as much preoccupied with him as he is with them.

Inevitably such religion is egoistic and superstitious, containing a good deal of myth, magic and miracle. But those who react against it have the option of progressing to the higher teachings which set out to counteract the eudaemonism of popular religion. At this higher level, religion becomes a discipline of disinterestedness. By following it I can learn to pass beyond self-concern and all the supernatural fears and fantasies that it creates.

Two-levelled religion may be accused of being too indulgent towards superstition, too complacent in its assumption that the religion of the common people will always be a kind of necessary illusion, and too easily used to legitimate a caste society. On the other hand it does have a certain resilience. When it meets philosophical criticism it can freely admit the naivety of popular religion. The real truth is in the higher teachings alone.

Christianity, however, is very reluctant to defend itself in this way by yielding its outworks and retreating to higher ground. On the contrary, it has always regarded its outworks of eudaemonism and supernaturalism as essential to it. It has been a highly theologized version of popular religion, and has a radical democratic strain in it which demands that the same faith be professed by every believer. There has always been a mystical élite influenced by neo-Platonism, and they have been allowed to get away with tacitly disregarding popular supernaturalism, but they have never been allowed openly to repudiate it. Christianity has always sensed that it cannot allow its outer walls to be breached without being in danger of losing the citadel. The whole system is seen as depending upon a sequence of mighty acts of God in a particular segment of past history. It is vital that each believer should feel that the entire supernatural world revolves about him personally, concentrates its entire attention upon him, watches, helps, admonishes and blesses him. Every moment of his life is invested with cosmic significance by the thought that his own soul and his daily behaviour are in the front line of a cosmic battle between good and evil supernatural powers. So it seemed quite natural to C. S. Lewis, and doubtless also to many of his readers, that he should *use* God, miracles and Hell to get revenge upon his opponents in the way he did.

This is not an outlook that can permit itself to be demythologized piecemeal. When Christian supernaturalism encounters criticism it fights to maintain itself intact. Like Islam, it has to be intellectually combative.

The battle has been long, but by now the old supernatural faith has become completely dissociated from the ways in which our modern secular culture has come to describe and explain the world. Once, physics depended upon a Prime Mover to instigate all changes in the universe, but modern physics does not. Once, life was a supernatural mystery to be explained only by the divine breathing of life into inert matter, but today life has been reduced to chemistry and chemistry to physics. Once, history and society were explained in terms of supernatural institution, validation, guidance, intervention and judgment, but nowadays all such ideas have dropped out and man is for good or ill the only maker of his own history and his own societies. In these and many other ways supernaturalist beliefs have ceased to play any constitutive part in any branch of knowledge. The clinching proof of it is that although there are still many supernaturalist believers about, none of them is putting forward or can possibly put forward any serious plans for reinstating supernaturalism in physics, agriculture, medicine and the rest. On the contrary, even the most extreme fundamentalists continue to make use of modern agricultural science, medicine, aeroplanes, television and so forth, just like everyone else. Their supernaturalism is still vociferously maintained, but in a psychologized and dissociated form. They profess to repudiate the underlying world-view of the society that they nevertheless continue to live off.

This spiritual hippiedom is becoming very common and very easy. The scientific and technological élite are few, knowledge has become very highly differentiated, and the machines have been made so simple to operate that most of us need not give a thought to the implications of the intellectual rigour and the

highly developed knowledge-systems that underlie the technolo-
gies we live by. At the popular level we are at liberty to believe any
nonsense we please. Modern society is becoming surprisingly
Hindu. There is a riot of popular belief-systems – amongst which
Christianity is now just one of many options – and they can all
flourish because of the general prosperity and forgetfulness created
by the small and largely concealed élite of intellectually disciplined
souls who maintain the scientific foundations of society. They
correspond to the thirty-six hidden saints of Jewish legend for
whose sake this crazy world is allowed to endure.

So there is now a double standard of intellectual virtue. At the
popular level eudaemonism prevails, often dignified by the name
of 'faith': people feel free to believe whatever they find helpful,
consoling and life-enriching. But before a new power-station, or
a new therapeutic drug, or a new aircraft may be brought into
regular use we are all of us agreed that it must be tested by an
altogether more stringent set of standards. Evidently we are all
aware that the higher standards do exist and we require the élite
to work to them, even though we would not dream of assessing
our own beliefs and daily practice by such strict criteria.

In this way the historic social position of the higher teachings
has been taken over by critical and scientific thinking, and a
strange psychology has grown up. We rely upon the élite but are
obscurely aware that their very existence is a reproach to our own
intellectual permissiveness. So we oblige them to keep quiet, tell
them they live in ivory towers out of touch with the real world,
resent them and try to forget about them – until we need them.
And this rather Freudian relationship between the masses and the
spiritual élite is a symptom of bad conscience.

What shall we say, then, to those who are quite content that
Christianity shall continue to exist and flourish on the low ground,
and join with everybody else in making rude noises about those
who live on the high ground? Only, that just as Christianity
cannot easily yield the low ground and retreat to the high, so also
it cannot readily yield the high ground and live only on the low. If
it does, it will suffer from bad conscience. Admittedly, only a few
people know what the high ground is like, but nowadays everybody knows that it exists and suspects that the world looks very
different from up there. If Christianity is to be at peace with itself,
then someone has to ask on what terms it is possible to be a

believer on the high ground, where the air is very thin and bracing nowadays.

There is an oft-quoted German saying to the effect that 'Only a Christian can be a good atheist; only an atheist can be a good Christian.' We can now see what it means. For their own souls' health Christians need to experience what life is like on the high ground today; and those whose calling it is to live habitually on the high ground need the help of the life-support systems of religion in order to survive. For the truth scarcely yet understood in the modern West is that the hard truth of the human situation as we are now coming to perceive it presents us with a *religious* problem and calls for a religious response. The pioneers who first climbed to the modern high ground were usually in revolt against religion as they understood it and so refused to acknowledge that they were confronted with a religious problem. They tended to stop short, frozen in attitudes of scepticism, pessimism or futile defiance. Nor have the religious been of the help they should be. Preoccupied with the work of defending an ancient world-view, and encouraging each other with the observation that at the popular level it does after all survive remarkably well (albeit with that element of bad conscience), they have not had time to address themselves to truthful religious reflection on the human situation as it now appears from the high ground. It is a respectable evangelical enterprise to go out and immerse oneself in the life-experience of a Third-World slum dweller or a factory worker, but it is not a respectable evangelical enterprise to attempt to climb to the high ground, because nobody wants to see just how much baggage has to be abandoned in the course of the ascent. In particular, nobody wants to look too closely at the intimate relation between Christian supernaturalism and eudaemonism, and traditional patterns of authority. The bargain is, 'Recognize my supernatural authority, and the more wholehearted and unquestioning your submission to me, the more deeply satisfying and reassuring to you will be my pledges to you of your personal supernatural protection and support.' Climbing to the high ground, we cannot help but see that bargain for what it is – something touching, and understandable, but entirely human – and supernaturalism falls away. Like St John of the Cross as he climbed his Mount Carmel, we are obliged to relinquish those particular consolations of religion.[9] We come to a region where the external world is an endless flux of phenomena, where we fully recognize that we can have no other point of view than our own, where we see that even the best knowledge available to us is still only provisional and of a status that is in principle uncertain. How are we to live in this climate? Four guiding principles become fundamental: truth, disinterestedness, creativity and love. Truth, because the old illusion-dominated views of the world and bases for living have inevitably been transcended; disinterestedness, because eudaemonistic consolations have been lost and we are left with the knowledge of our own transience; creativity, because no ready-built home for the spirit is provided and we have to build our own; and love, because the only way to give value to life is by each of us giving value to the others through disinterested love. Truth, disinterestedness, creativity, love: these principles have to be learnt, we have to become strong in them by a habitual, illusion-free practice of Christian faith just for its own sake, without the desire for power, without the desire to make any dubious bargains, and without either self-mutilation or the in-group/out-group psychology. We worship God as the symbolic personification of these guiding principles and ideal goals, and we see in Jesus a teacher of them and an embodiment of them; but we steadfastly refrain from claiming to have of God a kind of knowledge that human beings cannot have.

Here is a basis on which individuals can already begin to live an authentic modern Christian life; and it is not as novel as all that, for those in the past who set out upon the traditional way to God came in the end to much the same position.

For consider the logic of the traditional way to God. It was axiomatic that God is incomprehensible to the human mind and that we have no direct or immediate apprehension of him. All our knowledge of God is mediated by metaphors, symbols and analogies, none of them entirely adequate. However, we can get some guidance from two principles: the images can be arranged in a hierarchy such that by ascending the scale one can draw nearer to God; and secondly, each image has annexed to it a set of rules prescribing how it is to be used.

The rules for using the images are most important. Consider for example the difference between God's right hand and God's right arm. In the Bible God's right arm means his power exerted to gain the victory over his enemies, often Israel's enemies in battle. By contrast, talk of God's right hand refers to God's delegation of executive authority. It is the place occupied by his special representative or viceroy. The king of Israel, and later the ascended Christ, are represented as being seated at God's right hand. They are God's right-hand men. My right hand is more 'dexterous' than my left, and I use it for important tasks such as wielding a tool, a weapon or a pen. It is my prime agent that I use to accomplish my purposes. So a sovereign who delegates executive functions is as it were handing over the power of his right hand to his agent.

Thus talk of God's right arm is talk of God's power exerted to give or to gain victory, and talk of God's right hand is talk of God's delegation of power and authority. If we did not grasp the correct way of using the idioms, we might make the mistake of assembling them and fancying, perhaps, that God's right hand is on the end of God's right arm.

The relevance of all this becomes clear when we turn now to the lowest and simplest level of religious imagery, *physical anthropomorphism*. This way of speaking, common in the Old Testament but less common now, speaks of God in terms of parts of the human body. Thus we hear of God's face, eyes, eyelids, ears, lips, mouth, voice, right hand, right arm, left hand, heart and feet. If we assemble the imagery we might suppose that God is being thought of as having a human body, but in fact each idiom has its own distinctive and restricted use. Talk of God's face, for example, signifies his presence and attention to human needs. A petitioner who urgently sought audience of an ancient king had got what he desired when he came into the king's presence and the king graciously turned his countenance towards the suppliant. An Israelite going into the Jerusalem Temple was likewise seeking God's face.

There is a similar pattern of correct use associated with each of the other bodily metaphors. God's left hand is the place of condemnation, his feet and footstool are spoken of in connection with his enthronement over the world, and so on. It is clear that although these idioms have a useful part to play in religious language, the metaphors involved do not apply to God literally, or *proprie* as St Thomas Aquinas puts it.[10]

The next level up is *social anthropomorphism*, which speaks of God in terms of various social rôles. The most important are King, Judge, Father and Lord, and there is a subordinate group which includes such images as husband, shepherd, potter, vine-dresser, architect or builder, and modern examples like Galileo's engineer and mathematician. A great variety of trades and social rôles are ascribed to God, but they all imply some kind of leading, originative, creative and directing authority. Mediating and sub-ordinate rôles are not ascribed to God. Thus the Bible never calls God a prophet, priest or advocate, though these rôles are attribu-ted to Christ.

Again it is apparent that there must be rules prescribing the correct use of the image. For example, nobody would think it right to deduce from the image of God as Father that he has a consort or that he is our natural genitor. In fact in every case under this general heading the image is used to prescribe attitudes and behaviour. You should behave towards God as if he were your father, judge, king or lord. Piety is like an attitude of filial devotion; the devout man is as it were a plaintiff, a subject or a servant. Again the language about God is not descriptive and it is not to be assembled; its function is to guide piety and conduct along an appropriate path.

Ascending to the third level of religious language, we come now to *personal anthropomorphism*, which attributes to God various human intellectual and moral qualities. We hear of God's mind, thoughts, will, love, power, wisdom and goodness. This is a more refined way of speaking, but it is still anthropomorphic. It still draws elements from human life and experience and ascribes them to God, and there still have to be rules restricting the use of the images in order to prevent mistakes. If we take any one of the images too 'literally' we run into paradoxes. For example, talk of God's will has two main uses. Sometimes it is used as a way of persuading people to accept with resignation what has happened, as if everything that happens ought to be seen as an expression of God's will. But on other occasions we talk of finding out what it is God's will that we should do, as if 'what God wills' were just one of several future possibilities, among which we have a free choice. Now suppose that we take the idea of God's will descrip-tively and raise the question 'Can some things happen which God has *not* willed?' The answer must be No in terms of the first idiom, and Yes in terms of the other. Thus interpreting talk of God's will descriptively produces a contradiction, and we have to conclude that its meaning must be understood in terms of its uses. In the

former case it recommends an attitude to what is done and cannot
be undone, and in the latter case it guides our use of our freedom
of choice.

If along these lines we examine all the other personal and moral
qualities that are ascribed to God we find that there are rules
governing the use of each image, rules which prohibit us from
assembling the images into a composite portrait. Many theologians in the past certainly did try to assemble them, but the only
result was that they ran into all the old conundrums on which
rivers of ink have been spilt in vain down the centuries. If one is
more cautious and examines empirically the way the idioms work
in religious language, one must conclude that their function is to
shape piety and to set goals before us, but not to inform us.

St Thomas Aquinas claimed that the images were informative,
though in a Pickwickian sense.[11] For him language had originally
been taught to men by God, and it still retained the power to mean
heavenly things beyond the full comprehension of its merely
human speakers. We do not know what God's wisdom is, but
scripture authorizes us to speak of God as wise, and our words
say more than we can know they say. As it stands this doctrine is
scarcely sufficient. I can assure you that *Macardit ee nhialic* is a
meaningful theological utterance in the Dinka language (which it
is), and you may repeat the words after me and in a sense mean
more than you know you mean, but it will not be a profitable
exercise for you. Evidently Aquinas needs more than *that*, if he is
to justify his claim that the images give information. So he adds a
doctrine about causality: perfections that are found among crea-
tures may be inferred also to exist in an analogous but 'higher'
way in their Cause, because all causality is a communication of
being from greater to lesser. But we now have no good reason for
accepting either Aquinas' doctrine about causality[12] or his views
on the origin of language, and his argument to show that the
images are informative has therefore broken down.

So our ascent continues to the fourth and final level of religious
language and come at last to *images of boundlessness*, anti-images,
images of the unimaginable, images that dimly point beyond
language and the thinkable. They fall into two main groups.
Mystics speak of God as a shoreless sea, a darkness, a desert, an
abyss, a silence, a void and a mystery. Theologians use such
negative terms as infinite, incorporeal, impassible, incomprehen-

sible, immutable and so forth. It is true that these latter terms have often been handled in a naively confident dogmatic-metaphysical way, but their original function was to forbid such speculative arrogance. Often the language issues its warning by becoming consciously paradoxical, as when Henry Vaughan speaks of 'a deep but dazzling darkness',[13] or when God is spoken of as 'a circle whose centre is everywhere and whose circumference is nowhere'.[14] The resort to paradox shows that the writer has come to see that all the imagery through which he has been working his way is necessarily inadequate. The images signpost the path, but they do not describe its destination. Eventually the language autodestructs, and by doing so indirectly points to the Ineffable.

The final realization can be described in many ways, none of them satisfactory. We may say that in the end objectivity must be given up, and the highest happiness is to be gained only on the further side of that last and most difficult parting. Religion is a way of being rather than of knowing, and knowledge ultimately gives place to love, as the cherubim outrank the seraphim. Or we might say that theistic and non-theistic mysticism converge when it is grasped that the difference between theism and atheism cannot be stated in language – and in the end must not matter to us. Or we might say simply that everyone must eventually come to terms with his own transience and the Void that encircles him. Religion is about that; not about consolation, but first and foremost about the truth of life. You must enter what *The Cloud of Unknowing* calls a nothing and a nowhere, full blind and full dark.[15] In that emptiness eudaemonism is cauterized, and disinterested love becomes possible. It is divine bliss, but a world apart from the kind of consolation eudaemonism seeks.

I. B. Singer made the point very clear when he wrote an entire long novel for the sake of four words in the last line. The book tells of the last generations of a family of Polish Jews in the decades leading up to Hitler. Gradually it becomes clear to what end all the generations of tenacious living, hoping and waiting have been leading. There is to be no escape. 'The Messiah will come soon,' says Hertz Yanovar. His companion is surprised: 'What do you mean?' 'Death is the Messiah. That's the real truth.'[16]

Tolstoy similarly teaches the redemptive power of the fearsome encounter with death. At the end of his long agony Ivan Ilych is at last able to escape from self-concern and to repent enough to try to express concern for others. In that moment death vanishes. It is no more. He has eternal life – and he dies.[17]

We described the spiritual life in terms of an ascent through 'the divine names', the images of God, but the story would have had much the same plot if we had described instead the path taken by an ordinary believer who simply sets out to follow Jesus ethically all the way, even to the Cross. The truth of life being what it is, the pilgrim will be led along a path of much the same shape whatever his starting-point and method of travel. There is in human nature a little nerve of egoism, fearful self-concern, insatiable craving for security and horror of the Void, and it tends to organize the whole personality and our entire way of life around itself. For want of a better name let us call it sin. Whether it is strictly universal in human beings I do not know, but it seems to be near enough so, and strangely enough it is often the most respected institutions in society which pander to it the most. To cut that little nerve and become genuinely disinterested and carefree is very hard, and people resist it as they resist death itself. But we all know in our hearts that it must in the end be cut, for life itself – or rather, the inescapable presence of death in life as part of life – teaches us so; and cutting it is a miraculous deliverance, as if one had passed through death to a new and divine life beyond it.

Here, then, is a basis on which religion can be practised and life can become blessed for those who live on what we called the high ground. But Christianity is not concerned merely with providing a mysticism for the élite: it is a social faith, and its perennial hope for a better world is logically prior to its message to the individual. In this connection we have been arguing that the modern Western culture which has now spread across the whole globe is the product of a sceptical, critical, scientific and demythologizing spirit which we called the will to truth. The will to truth heightens consciousness, relentlessly unmasks illusions, questions established tradition and authority, and undermines everything that whole peoples have hitherto lived by. Because it regards truth not as something inherited and dogmatically possessed, but as an ideal goal to which at best one may only hope gradually to approximate, it travels very light indeed, much lighter than most people hitherto have thought tolerable.

Traditional societies depended upon a vision of the world as a given, enduring sacred order, and the supernatural realm was confidently postulated as the cause of that order. People did not worry so much about the nature of knowledge, for they were confident that they possessed it; the mind simply conformed itself to and accepted a given sacred reality. It was customary to hold that there was such a thing as absolute knowledge, whether gained by metaphysical thinking or by revelation or just from tradition, and that possession of this knowledge conferred blessedness. Indeed it might, if it could be had; but absolute metaphysical knowledge could only be attained if it were possible to step right outside the limits of language and thought and see the world from an absolute point of view, and critical thinking shows the meaninglessness of such an idea. As for knowledge by revelation, once critical ways of thinking have become firmly established it becomes impossible to see how knowledge could be implanted in us ready-made, on a plate, in a way that by-passes and is exempt from the normal limitations of our language and thinking. We can no longer see clearly what such supernaturally-bestowed knowledge could consist in, or how we could assimilate it so that it could become truly *ours* and be put to use by us.

A culture that has become critical, then, has given up the idea of absolute knowledge and is even cautious about claims to objective knowledge of this world. It is perforce content to travel light. No longer able to look up to a real supernatural world above, it instead projects the better world and the better self that it seeks forwards, as goals of ethical striving. The better world is not a world above but a world to come. Religious objects will thus be seen not as metaphysical beings above us, but as ideals or postulates which supply us with goals to inspire action and principles to guide it. It used to be thought that religious belief expresses a kind of picturesque metaphysics, but instead it must now be seen as offering a path to spiritual perfection to the individual and to the community. The religious and cultural crisis towards which the will to truth has led us may thus be seen as the birthpangs of the Kingdom of God. The demythologizing of the ancient religions and the breakdown of the old foundation of the moral order is leading us to a time when we will have to choose the new world, because no other possibility remains to us.

Thus although we have renounced one form of dualism, that which distinguishes between this world below and the supernatural world above, we are still affirming another which contrasts

the present age with an age to come. And here we run into a storm
of criticism. Some say that messianic and utopian dreams of a
perfect society, seductive though they are, are profoundly mis-
guided.[18] When people in the past set out to try to realize them
they always ended in disaster if they failed or in tyranny when
they succeeded. A gradualist approach that sets out to identify
and reduce particular evils one by one is more realistic and has
been proved in practice. More fundamentally, there is a strong
tradition of tough-minded biological naturalism which maintains
that the human drives are what they are and it is folly to pretend
that they can ever be otherwise. This tradition, reaching back to
Hobbes and Machiavelli, usually considers that the best we can
expect to see is that the irrational and antisocial impulses in
human nature will be curbed and controlled by a strong government. Hobbes even identifies the Kingdom of God – at least until
the Second Coming – with the Christian sovereign's absolute rule
over his subjects.[19]

A line of Christian thinkers, going back beyond Luther to
Augustine and perhaps even to St Paul, have accepted this
pessimistic view of human nature and what could be made of it.
Our present social life is a cultural construction which has been
achieved by disciplining, redirecting, symbolically transforming
and sublimating our raw biological drives. Thus the primitive
desire for vengeance is transformed into a penal system; male
aggression, territoriality and desire for sexual power are transformed into patriarchal marriage and property-law; and the
solidarity of a kin-group is extended and transformed into patri-
otism and allegiance to one's nation. But these cultural transforms
of raw impulse need both symbolic disguises to conceal their
lowly origins and the threat of force to maintain their authority.
So religion comes to culture's aid and backs it up with validating
myths. The work of grace is not to destroy nature but to perfect
it; which means that since human nature remains at bottom the
same and is not going to change while history endures, religion
must recognize that no better option is available than to work
upon the given materials with the traditional tools. As for the
hope of a new kind of human being and a new basis for social life,
that must await the end of the world.

Some modern movements – Marxism, anarchism, nineteenth-
century liberalism – have believed that the perfect society was

historically attainable, but their conception of it was often religiously weak, and they were upborne by an illusory belief in progress. On the other hand, those whose idea of the *Summum Bonum* (the highest good) was more adequate and who were more realistic, figures such as Kant and the Christian moralist Reinhold Niebuhr,[20] regarded the Kingdom of God as a regulative ideal, always influencing us but never actually realizable in history.

I have argued both for a religiously-strong conception of the Kingdom of God and for the need to realize it historically; and this may seem to be a bad case of trying to have it both ways. But my claim has been that the will to truth has now exposed and demystified all the traditional mechanisms by which nature has been converted into culture. For example, the cultural and religious idealization of bourgeois patriarchal marriage reached its greatest heights in Victorian Britain just at the moment when it was about to be subjected to a merciless critical analysis and demystification which still continues and now obliges us to rethink all our ideas about the relations of men and women from the very beginning. Or again, the nation still has biological roots: it is a confederation of tribes which are in turn sets of interrelated descent-groups, and it is still a society of people who are prepared to shed their blood for each other because they feel they are of one blood. The nation still proclaims itself sovereign and a complete moral world to its members, and even yet almost no serious concession has been made to the principle that in cases of clear conflict the wider claim of humanity as a whole can and should override merely national loyalties. Treason remains the worst crime. Yet people know that the nation-state is historically obsolete. A conscientious objector to military service, a scientist who judges that his work should be openly published to all the world and not be kept secret for the sake of national security, a statesman who seeks disarmament and the redistribution of the world's wealth – all of them know that the old view that the national interest is the highest natural moral claim on us is no longer defensible. Twice this century after major wars there have been attempts to set up a supra-national authority with real powers. They failed; but sooner or later we must transcend nationalism if we are to survive.

In ways like these the received moral order inherited from tradition and sanctified by religion has disintegrated in modern times. It has lost moral authority and in many cases has even become highly objectionable, and it belongs to a past when people lived within narrow myths that have now died. The questioning runs deeper. We begin to doubt the traditional models of nature, culture and their relations, and their implied comparison of man with an animal that must be improved by domestication. We wonder about the ancient mythological contrast between the wild and the tame that still governs our thinking about these issues, especially now we have learnt that our animal cousins are not in fact so brutal, bestial, ferocious and savage as they were portrayed. Perhaps the very image of nature as violent and disorderly, still accepted by Freud, was itself an ideological fiction, a bogeyman invented by the powers that be in order to persuade us to accept their authority and be good children?

When critical analysis thus begins to expose the power-interests that have shaped our basic concepts, concepts such as those of nature, culture and sacred authority, we become more and more uncertain as to where and how we are to lay the foundations for a reconstruction of the moral order. My argument that the times are leading us to seek a wholly fresh start, a new understanding of religion and a new basis for social life, will seem intelligible only insofar as you are led to agree with me that the old order is decayed so far that we are being *forced* to begin all over again. How are we to do this? I have claimed that in Jesus, in his relation to the Judaism of his day, in his prophetic message about the Kingdom of God and in his death, we can find in condensed form a relevant diagnosis, and a still-unfulfilled possibility of a new world. Perhaps we may find that people at large do after all have capacities for spiritual freedom, for disinterestedness and for altruism which the old ideologies denied them. Perhaps the new world is not 'impossible', as it has been called, but is practically necessary and close at hand.

Notes

Introduction

1. 'A Free Man's Worship' (1903), reprinted in *Mysticism and Logic*, 1918; reprinted Penguin Books 1953, p. 51.

2. See N. C. Gillespie, *Charles Darwin and the Problem of Creation*, Chicago University Press 1979, for an account of the transition from theological science to positive science with special reference to Darwin.

3. See A. H. Basson, *David Hume*, Penguin Books 1958, pp. 20ff., for illuminating comments on the idea of absolute knowledge and Hume's criticism of it.

4. Compare Thomas Nagel, *Mortal Questions*, Cambridge University Press 1979, especially Essays 2 and 14.

5. Ludwig Feuerbach, *Thoughts on Death and Immortality* (1830), trans. James A. Massey, University of California Press, Berkeley, 1980, is the classic critique of Christian eudaemonism.

6. This view of religious language, familiar today through the writings of D. Z. Phillips and others, has a long history. It first appeared as a widely-held position in the generation after John Locke. The Deists had criticized the traditional external evidences of Christianity (the arguments from prophecy and miracle), and also complained that it was impossible to believe doctrines, such as that of the Trinity, which could not be understood. In reply orthodox apologists as varied as Peter Browne, Robert Jenkin and George Berkeley laid increased emphasis on the 'internal evidence' of Christianity, meaning its appeal to conscience. They admitted that the Trinity is strictly incomprehensible, but argued that accepting it has valuable moral and religious effects. We may call this 'theological pragmatism', the view that the truth of dogmas consists in their effectiveness in producing holiness, and that their meaning is given by the way they are used in practice. Modern theology would be greatly benefitted if we possessed a full history and a philosophical analysis of theological pragmatism, because in various disguised forms – for example, in talk of 'orthopraxis' – it is becoming more and more common today. Historically, we observe that theological pragmatism tends to appear at

times when the dominant philosophy of the day stresses the limits of thought or language and so appears to preclude any speculative grasp of religious truth.

7. *The Will to Power*, ed. Walter Kaufmann, Vintage Books, New York 1968, e.g. §§17–20, §30, §253, etc.

8. P. T. Geach, *Truth, Love and Immortality: An Introduction to McTaggart's Philosophy*, Cambridge 1979, p. 25.

9. On this point see my 'Kant and the Negative Theology', in *The Philosophical Frontiers of Christian Theology*, ed. B. L. Hebblethwaite and S. R. Sutherland, Cambridge University Press 1982.

1 Hyperborean Faith

1. *The Antichrist*, §1.

2. David A. Pailin, 'Theology', in *The Twentieth-Century Mind*, ed. C. B. Cox and A. E. Dyson, Vol. III, Oxford University Press 1972, p. 104.

3. John H. S. Kent, 'Christian Theology in the Eighteenth to Twentieth Centuries', in, *A History of Christian Doctrine*, ed. H. Cunliffe-Jones, T. & T. Clark 1978, pp. 459–591, reissued as *The End of the Line? The Development of Christian Theology in the Last Two Centuries*, SCM Press 1982.

4. *Les mots et les choses*, Gallimard, Paris 1966; ET *The Order of Things*, Tavistock Press 1970. See also Alan Sheridan, *Michel Foucault: The Will to Truth*, Tavistock Press 1980.

5. *The Origin of Species*, Chapter XIV.

6. *Beyond Good and Evil*, §296. Even Nietzsche's own thoughts quickly decay into banality as he writes them down.

7. Arthur C. Danto, *Nietzsche as Philosopher*, Columbia University Press, New York 1980, p. 110n.

8. From Nietzsche's posthumously published fragment, *Concerning Truth and Falsehood in an Extra-Moral Sense* (1873). The translation is Arthur C. Danto's.

9. F. W. Nietzsche, *The Will to Power*, §480, ed. W. Kaufmann, Vintage Books, New York 1968, p. 266.

10. William Chillingworth, *The Religion of Protestants* (1637), ii. 82.

11. F. W. Nietzsche, *Concerning Truth and Falsehood in an Extra-Moral Sense* (1873).

12. Richard H. Popkin, *The History of Scepticism from Erasmus to Spinoza*, University of California Press 1979.

13. E.g. I Cor. 3.1f.; Heb. 5.12ff.; II Cor. 3.6; Gal. 3.24f.

14. In *Taking Leave of God*, SCM Press 1980.

15. See Gershon Weiler, *Mauthner's Critique of Language*, Cambridge University Press 1970.

2 Religious Change and the Politics of Truth

1. *Proceedings of the Aristotelian Society* 1944–45, and many times reprinted.

2. 'Eternal Life', in *Talk of God* (Royal Institute of Philosophy Lectures 1967–68), ed. G. N. A. Vesey, Macmillan 1969, pp. 239–50.

3. For example, I. M. Crombie's contribution to *Faith and Logic*, ed. Basil Mitchell, Allen and Unwin 1957, and Mitchell's contribution to the symposium cited in n. 4 below.

4. 'Theology and Falsification', in *New Essays in Philosophical Theology*, ed. A. G. N. Flew and A. C. MacIntyre, SCM Press 1955, pp. 99–103; and 'Religion and Morals', in *Faith and Logic*, cited above.

5. 'The Groundlessness of Belief', in *Reason and Religion*, ed. Stuart C. Brown, Cornell University Press, Ithaca 1977, pp. 143–57.

6. *An Empiricist's View of the Nature of Religious Belief*, Cambridge University Press 1955.

7. *Religion and the Scientific Outlook*, Allen and Unwin 1959.

8. *Religious Experience*, Macmillan 1972.

9. 'Religion and Morals', in *Faith and Logic* (n. 4 above), pp. 186f. Compare C. C. J. Webb, 'The idolatry of today is often the true religion of yesterday, and the true religion of today the idolatry of tomorrow', *God and Personality*, Allen and Unwin 1918, p. 164.

10. Among Phillips' writings see especially *The Concept of Prayer*, Routledge 1965, reprinted Blackwell 1981; *Faith and Philosophical Enquiry*, Routledge 1970; and *Religion without Explanation*, Blackwell 1976.

11. Patrick Collinson, *Archbishop Grindal*, Cape 1979, pp. 153ff.

12. W. K. Clay, *Liturgies and Occasional Forms of Prayer Set Forth in the Reign of Queen Elizabeth*, Parker Society, Cambridge 1847, esp. pp. 567ff.

13. Thomas Kendrick, *The Lisbon Earthquake*, Methuen 1956.

14. Owen Chadwick, *The Secularization of the European Mind in the Nineteenth Century*, Cambridge University Press 1975, pp. 259ff.

15. John Hick, *God and the Universe of Faiths*, Macmillan 1973.

16. John Hick (ed.), *The Myth of God Incarnate*, SCM Press 1977.

17. See, for example, John Drury, *The Pot and the Knife*, SCM Press 1979.

18. *Jesus and the Gospel of God*, Lutterworth Press 1979; *Taking Leave of God*, SCM Press 1980.

19. See Horton Harris, *David Friedrich Strauss and his Theology*, Cambridge 1973, pp. 259ff., which draws upon the fuller account in C. Hartlichs and W. Sachs, *Der Ursprung des Mythosbegriffes in der modernen Bibelwissenschaft*, Tübingen 1952.

20. Herbert Weisinger, cited in T. J. J. Altizer and William Hamilton, *Radical Theology and the Death of God*, Penguin Books 1968, p. 169.

21. *The Life of Jesus Critically Examined*, translated by George Eliot and edited by Peter C. Hodgson, reissued SCM Press and Fortress Press, Philadelphia 1973, p. 673, etc.

22. Cited by Maurice Wiles in *The Myth of God Incarnate*, p. 153.

23. Some are reviewed in G. S. Kirk, *Myth: Its Meaning and Functions in Ancient and Other Cultures*, Cambridge University Press 1970.

24. 'Myth in Theology', in *The Myth of God Incarnate* (nn. 16, 22 above).

25. Op.cit., pp. 159f.

26. Ibid., p. 165.

27. E.g. Richard Rorty, *Philosophy and the Mirror of Nature*, Blackwell 1980.

28. See Renford Bambrough legislating in this way in *Reason and Religion* (n. 5 above), pp. 13–19.

3 The Message that Cannot be Understood

1. From the 'Diapsalmata' at the beginning of *Either/Or* (1843). Translated by D. F. and L. M. Swenson, Doubleday Anchor Books, New York 1959, Volume 1, p. 30.

2. Ezek. 2.5–7; 3.11.

3. Ezek. 3.7f.

4. Ezek. 33.32.

5. Ezek. 3–5.

6. Ezek. 12.

7. Ezek. 24.

8. Ezek. 20.49.

9. Ezek. 24.26f.

10. Peter Brook, *The Empty Space*, Penguin Books 1972, p. 79.

11. John Arden, *Sergeant Musgrave's Dance*, Methuen 1960.

12. E.g. Matt. 13.34.

13. Mark 4.10–12.

14. Mark 3.21f.

15. *Ecce Homo* (1889), 'Why I am a Destiny', 1.

16. E.g. *Human, All-too-Human* (1878), §84, 'The Prisoners'. Notice the curious resemblance between this parable and Kafka's 'In a Penal Colony'. In both cases it is implied that Christ already knew that God is dead.

17. §125.

18. 'Mut', No. 22 in the song-cycle: 'Will kein Gott auf Erdensein/Sind wir selber Götter'.

19. Walter Kaufmann's translation in his *The Portable Nietzsche*, Viking Press 1954, pp. 95f.

20. ET Kegan Paul, Trench, Trubner 1895, Vol. III, pp. 86f.

21. ET John Snodgrass, Beacon Press, Boston 1959, p. 103.

22. *The Attack on Christendom*, trans. W. Lowrie, Princeton 1944; and see John W. Elrod, *Kierkegaard and Christendom*, Princeton 1981.

23. *The Genealogy of Morals*, 1887, 3, xxvii.

24. *The Sickness Unto Death*, W. Lowrie, Doubleday Anchorbooks, New York 1954, p. 174.

25. Cited by Raymond Duval in 'The Uniqueness of the Individual and the Solitude of Becoming', in *Nietzsche and Christianity*, Concilium 124, ed. Claude Geffré and J. P. Jossua, T. & T. Clark 1981, p. 27 (my italics).

26. *Concluding Unscientific Postscript*, trans. D. F. Swenson and W. Lowrie, Princeton University Press 1941, p. 542.

27. X^2 A 299; but note that Kierkegaard is still careful to ascribe the doctrine to his pseudonym 'Johannes Climacus'.

28. See Andrew J. Burgess, *Passion, 'Knowing How' and Understanding:*

An Essay on the Concept of Faith (American Academy of Religion Dissertation Series no. 9), Scholars Press, Missoula, Montana 1975.

29. From *On Truth and Lie in an Extra-Moral Sense* (1873). Compare the similar story in *Five Prefaces to Five Unwritten Books*, 1(1872).

30. David Hume, *A Treatise of Human Nature*, Book 1(1739), ed. L. A. Selby-Bigge, Oxford 1878, and many subsequent editions, p. 183.

31. Ibid., p. 179.

32. *Dialogues Concerning Natural Religion* (1779), ed. N. Kemp Smith, Collins 1947, p. 135.

33. *Treatise*, p. 266.

34. *Thus Spoke Zarathustra* I, 'On the Thousand and One Goals'.

35. Ibid., 'On the Three Metamorphoses'.

36. *The Anti-Christ* (1888, published 1895), §32.

37. *The Anti-Christ*, §28.

38. There is good fierce polemic on this point in Dorothee Sölle, *Suffering* ET Darton, Longman and Todd 1975, ch. 1, 'A Critique of Christian Masochism'.

39. E.g. R. H. Dalitz, in *Nature*, Vol. 284, No. 5758 (24 April 1980), pp. 679f.

40. Expositions by leading authorities are to be found in *Scientific American*: Howard Georgi (Vol. 244, No. 4, April 1981) and Steven Weinberg (Vol. 244, No. 6, June 1981).

41. Bernard Lovell, *In the Centre of Immensities*, Hutchinson 1979, is a judicious survey.

42. Reprinted in P. B. Medawar, *The Art of the Soluble*, Methuen 1967, pp. 71–84.

43. See the discussion in Lloyd Geering, *Faith's New Age*, Collins 1980, esp. pp. 105f.

4 Christ (I): Gathering up the Fragments

1. As recollected by his wife Georgette, in René Passeron, *René Magritte*, Filipacci, New York 1980, p. 12.

2. Ibid., p. 36.

3. There is an account of Mondrian's background in an essay by Herbert Henkels in *Mondrian and the Hague School*, Whitworth Art Gallery, Manchester 1980, pp. 51ff.

4. See my *Taking Leave of God*, passim.

5. D. F. Strauss, *Der Christus des Glaubens und der Jesus der Geschichte*, Berlin 1865.

5 Christ (II): The Ironist

1. Joachim Jeremias, *New Testament Theology*, Vol. 1, SCM Press 1971, pp. 14ff. Jeremias lists 138 instances in the synoptic tradition.

2. *The Concept of Irony* (1841), with a useful summary and discussion in

George E. Arbaugh and George B. Arbaugh, *Kierkegaard's Authorship*, Allen and Unwin 1968, pp. 47–58.

3. *The Clouds*, line 226. Plato was sufficiently irritated by this to make Socrates reply to it at length in the *Apology*, 18E–24B.

4. This satirical note led me in *Jesus and the Gospel of God* (Lutterworth Press 1979, pp. 62ff.) mistakenly to characterize Jesus' method as humorous rather than ironical.

5. For example, in *The Genealogy of Morals* (1887), 3, xxvii; elaborating an idea outlined in §357 of *The Gay Science*, Book Five (written in 1886).

6. A. von Harnack, *Marcion*, Berlin 1921, passim.

6 Christ (III): The Saviour

1. The limitations of doctrinal arguments based on Jesus' personality and character are persuasively pointed out by D. E. Nineham in his 'Epilogue' to *The Myth of God Incarnate*, pp. 186–204.

2. John Hick uses an argument of this kind to prove God's existence in *The Centre of Christianity*, SCM Press 1977, pp. 48–55.

3. Gerald O'Collins SJ, *Fundamental Theology*, Darton, Longman and Todd 1981, pp. 86f., has an argument of this type. He claims that the Old Testament experience of God is so noble that it could only have been acquired through an authentic revelation of God.

4. A. T. Hanson and R. P. C. Hanson, *Reasonable Belief*, Oxford University Press 1980, p. 63.

5. Ibid., p. 65.

6. E.g. E. E. Evans-Pritchard, *Nuer Religion*, Oxford University Press 1956, ch. 11; R. de Vaux, *Ancient Israel*, Darton, Longman and Todd 1961, Part IV, chs. 10–13.

7. Excellent discussions in Evans-Pritchard, op. cit., ch. VII; and especially in Mary Douglas, *Purity and Danger*, Penguin Books 1970, and *Natural Symbols*, Penguin Books 1973.

8. *The Gay Science* (1882), §135. Nietzsche mistakenly thinks that there is something peculiarly Jewish about such ideas.

9. Sir Thomas Browne, *Religio Medici* (1642), Part the Second §11.

10. E.g. F. R. Tennant, *The Origin and Propagation of Sin*, Cambridge University Press 1902, and *The Concept of Sin*, Cambridge University Press 1912.

11. E.g. Evans-Pritchard, op.cit., p. 189.

12. The best survey is still R. S. Franks, *The Work of Christ* (1918), reprinted Nelson 1962.

13. R. C. Moberley, *Atonement and Personality*, John Murray 1901. Until recently this book has been very greatly admired. It is a sign of how rapidly we are changing that it now looks so sinister.

14. 'The Conception of the Kingdom of God in the Transformation of Eschatology' (1960), first published in English in E. N. Mozley's *The Theology of Albert Schweitzer*; reprinted in *Religion from Tolstoy to Camus*, ed. Walter Kaufmann, Harper Torchbooks, New York 1964, p. 409.

15. *The Anti-Christ* (written 1888, published 1895), §41.

16. Matt. 21.31.
17. E.g. *The Will to Power*, §174 (1887–8).
18. William Temple, *Christus Veritas*, Macmillan 1924, p. 161.
19. Michael Argyle and Benjamin Beit-Hallahmi, *The Social Psychology of Religion*, Routledge 1975, reviews the results of some 700 research reports.
20. G. E. W. Scobie, *Psychology of Religion*, Batsford 1975, p. 76.
21. Argyle, op.cit., pp. 87f., 148ff.
22. Ibid., pp. 108ff., 112ff.
23. Evidence in Argyle and Scobie, and see also Derek Wright, *The Psychology of Moral Behaviour*, Penguin Books 1971, especially pp. 229ff.
24. Argyle, ch. 6, passim.
25. Argyle, ch. 7, passim.
26. Argyle, op.cit., pp. 113f.
27. Ibid., pp. 113, 117f.
28. Scobie makes more of this distinction than does Argyle.
29. Argyle, op.cit., p. 115.
30. Beatrice Webb, *My Apprenticeship*, Longmans 1929, p. 123.
31. S. Kierkegaard, *Works of Love* (1847).

7 Christ (IV): The New Humanity

1. See the comments on Mark 3.19b–35 by D. E. Nineham, *St Mark*, Penguin Books 1963, pp. 118–25, and Geza Vermes, *Jesus the Jew*, Fontana Books 1976, pp. 33f.
2. J. A. T. Robinson, *Twelve New Testament Studies*, SCM Press 1962, pp. 139–53. The case is based mainly on Acts 3.13–26.
3. I Cor. 11.23–26.
4. In spite of the contrary view defended by Joachim Jeremias, *The Eucharistic Words of Jesus*, SCM Press 1966.
5. A. O. Lovejoy, *The Great Chain of Being*, Harvard University Press 1936, Ch. IV, etc.
6. Hans Küng, *Does God Exist?*, Collins 1980, pp. 656, 658.
7. D. F. Strauss, *The Life of Jesus Critically Examined* (1835), SCM Press 1973, p. 784.
8. Albert Schweitzer, *The Quest of the Historical Jesus* (1906), A. & C. Black 1954. p. 397.
9. Ibid., p. 400.
10. From 'The Conception of the Kingdom of God in the Transformation of Eschatology', in *Religion from Tolstoy to Camus*, ed. Walter Kaufmann, Harper Torchbooks, New York 1964, p. 424.
11. F. W. Nietzsche, *Twilight of the Idols* (1888), chs. 3, 4; *The Will to Power*, ed. Walter Kaufmann, Vintage Books, New York 1968 §§2–28 (written 1887–8).
12. John Stuart Mill, 'The Utility of Religion', written in the late 1850s and first published posthumously in *Nature, the Utility of Religion, Theism* (1874). See the opening paragraphs.
13. *The Will to Power*, §1.

14. Ibid., §12.

15. Ibid., §15.

16. E.g. Alasdair MacIntyre, *After Virtue*, Duckworth 1981, pp. 71f.

17. *Dichtung und Wahrheit*, Part III (1814), Book 14, p. 442. (See Walter Kaufmann's note on this in his footnote to §141 of Nietzsche's *The Gay Science*, Vintage Books, New York 1974, p. 190.)

8 Passing through the Fire

1. For Durkheim's theory of religion see Emile Durkheim, *The Elementary Forms of the Religious Life*, Allen and Unwin 1915. Brief account in Anthony Giddens, *Durkheim*, Fontana Books 1978, ch. 5.

2. Matt. 20.20–28; Luke 22.24–27, etc.

3. Matt. 6.2–18.

4. E.g. Matt. 18.15–18.

5. Cited by Maurice Wiles in *Incarnation and Myth: The Debate Continued*, ed. Michael Gouldcr, SCM Press 1979, p. 9.

6. R. W. Southern, *Western Society and the Church in the Middle Ages*, Penguin Books 1970, pp. 34–44.

7. For this and its implications see R. H. Popkin, *A History of Scepticism from Erasmus to Spinoza*, University of California Press, Berkeley 1979, ch. 1.

8. The modern concept of male homosexuality was invented in 1895 by Havelock Ellis and 'lesbianism' some twenty years later. See Lilian Faderman, *Surpassing the Love of Men*, Junction Books 1981.

9 G. E. Moore, *Principia Ethica*, Cambridge University Press 1903.

10. E.g. Mary Warnock, *Ethics since 1900*, Oxford University Press 1960, ch. 2; Philippa Foot (ed.), *Theories of Ethics*, Oxford University Press 1967, I-VIII.

11. *The Will to Power*, §12.

12. Arthur C. Danto, *Nietzsche as Philosopher*, Columbia University Press, New York 1980, ch. 8. I again commend this book as an exceptionally clear exposition.

13. David Hume, *A Treatise of Human Nature*, Book 1 (1739), Part IV, § vii.

14. Ludwig Wittgenstein, *Tractatus Logico-Philosophicus* (1922), ET by D. F. Pears and B. F. McGuinness, Routledge 1961. 5.621, 5.63, 5.62.

15. Ibid., 6.431.

16. Richard M. Titmuss, *The Gift Relationship*, Allen and Unwin 1970, p. 89.

17. Ibid., chs., 7, 13.

18. *After Virtue* (ch. 7, n. 16 above), passim.

19. For example, the four 'Formless Jhanas' in Theravadin mediation, as described in Daniel Goleman, *Varieties of the Meditative Experience*, Rider 1978, Part One; and briefly, but very clearly, in Ninian Smart, *Background to the Long Search*, BBC Publications 1977, pp. 63ff.

9 *The New World*

1. Hearsay: my informant is an Oxford theologian.

2. *Doctrine in the Church of England*, SPCK 1938, reprinted 1962.

3. *Christian Believing*, SPCK 1976.

4. *Believing in the Church*, SPCK 1981.

5. Peter Hebblethwaite, *The New Inquisition?*, Collins 1980.

6. E.g. R. N. Bellah, 'Religious Evolution', *American Sociological Review* 29, 1964, pp. 358–74; reprinted in Roland Robertson (ed.), *Sociology of Religion*, Penguin Books 1969, pp. 262–92.

7. Ibid., p. 289.

8. *Leviathan*, Part One, ch. 4.

9. See Gerald Brenan, *St John of the Cross*, Cambridge University Press 1974, Plate 4. The 'heavenly goods' on the pilgrim's left hand must be avoided from the very beginning of his journey.

10. *Summa Theologiae*, 1a, 13, 3.

11. *Summa Theologiae*, Vol. 3, ed. Herbert McCabe, Blackfriars 1964, passim.

12. E.g. Anthony Kenny, *The Five Ways*, Routledge 1969.

13. Henry Vaughan (1621/2–1695), 'The Night', line 50.

14. St Bonaventure uses this phrase in his *Itinerarium*, but I do not know who originated it.

15. *The Cloud of Unknowing* (fourteenth century, anon), ch. 68.

16. Isaac Bashevis Singer, *The Family Moskat*, trans. A. H. Gross, Penguin Books 1980, p. 634.

17. Leo Tolstoy, *The Cossacks and Other Stories*, trans. Rosemary Edmonds, Penguin Books 1960, pp. 160f.

18. K. R. Popper, *The Open Society and its Enemies*, Routledge 1945; John Passmore, *The Perfectibility of Man*, Duckworth 1970.

19. *Leviathan*, Part Three, chs. 32–43.

20. *An Interpretation of Christian Ethics*, SCM Press 1936.

Index of Names

Elijah - 16a.